WISDOM
FROM THE
WILD HEART

WISDOM
FROM THE
WILD HEART

WISDOM FROM THE WILD HEART

Ordering information: Quantity Sales. Special discounts are available on quantity purchases by corporations, associations, and others. For details, contact the Special Sales Department at Visionary Insight Press.

Visionary Insight Press
913 Beal Parkway NW Suite A #117
Fort Walton Beach, FL 32547

Visionary Insight Press, the Visionary Insight Press logo and its individual parts are trademarks of Visionary Insight Press.

Compiled by: Katina F Gillespie

Back cover photo credit: John J Kelly, Kendal Vaughan / VonRoe design, Distel Photography, Austring Photography, Alicia Schuette Photography & Conversions, Jase White, Jeanette Dreyer, Heidi Phillips, ASM Studio, Alimond Studios, Diane Stoppard Photography, Katy Moses Photography, Charles Ferrell, Paige Rudolph, Lauren VanNatta, Nicole Ryan Photography, Courtney Pullman

Don't limit yourself. Many
people limit themselves to
what they think they can do.
You can go as far as your mind
lets you. What you believe,
remember, you can achieve.

~ MARY KAY ASH

Table of Contents

Foreword

by Katina Gillespie

 Make voyages! Attempt them! There's nothing else.

~ TENNESSEE WILLIAMS

M ost of our life we are advised to live cautiously. To buckle our seat belts. To look both ways before crossing a street. To save money. To stay in school. To eat healthy foods. To get regular checkups. Avoiding foolish risks is, of course, good advice. Still, we are unable to grow unless we take some risks. Occasionally we need to take advantage of one of the adventures that life offers … Live it up and live in the now! Free to express ourselves.

This compilation holds dear to my heart as I have been known to take the road less travelled and taking risks that did not seem to be wise now. My personal journey has had many twists and turns, peaks and valleys but somehow I have prevailed and come out with wisdom and courage to face another day.

Life often delivers adversity that we could never imagine but in what appears to be weakness or fear at first, proves to deliver strength and courage. It is in our darkest hour that we find our true colors and shine the brightest. Visionary Insight Press honors all paths to enlightenment and beliefs as we welcome individual voices. The authors in this project share experiences that are uplifting, inspiring, and diverse but all of them find the underlying lessons and wisdom that life brings forward. We all encounter various setbacks and successes. In fact, it may be necessary to encounter both disappointment and triumph, so that we can know who we are, what we can rise from, and how we can come out of it.

Most of us have it all wrong! We are the authors of our own life. We didn't come here to master unconditional love. That is where we come from and where we will return. We came here to learn individual love. Universal love. Messy love. Sweaty love. Crazy love. Broken love. Whole love that is infused with divinity and lived through the grace of stumbling. It is demonstrated through the beauty of…messing up. You are not here to be perfect. You already are! You came here to be beautifully human; flawed and fabulous.

Each author shares a moment, situation, occurrence, or belief that left them wiser than before. *Wisdom From the Wild Heart* is a collection of adventures of when the authors took a leap of faith, against all odds, and came out shining brighter than ever imagined. They provide a gift of inspiration to encourage others to spread their wings and take flight! As you read this collection of talented authors from all around the globe, you will find inner confidence and soar to your highest potential.

You were born to be limitless! Once you embrace this, you will create possibilities! As these authors share powerful moments in their lives that inspired them to step outside their comfort zone and experience understanding, confidence, strength and awareness, you will be transformed. We have the choice to curl up in a ball and be a victim, go through life ignoring the beauty that surrounds, or get up in the morning with a smile and realize that there are obstacles in life and it's how you deal with them that determines success and inner peace.

Enjoy the adventure as you experience wisdom from wild hearts!

Namaste,
Katina Gillespie
www.EmotionalHarmonyWellness.com

Feel The *Pulse*

Saturday night party
Feel the *Pulse* of anticipation
      Dancing and laughing
      Feel the *Pulse* of friendship
            Watching the performers
            Feel the *Pulse* of fun
                Shots ring out
                Feel the *Pulse* of fear
            Friends are dying
            Feel the *Pulse* of panic
      Mother saves her child
      Feel the *Pulse* of ultimate love
Couples dying together
Feel the *Pulse* of soul mates
      One man gives his life to save his partner
      Feel the *Pulse* of true love
            One man steps up to help save dozens
            Feel the *Pulse* of bravery
      One man risks his life to save a stranger
      Feel the *Pulse* of compassion
            A parent's worst nightmare
            Feel the *Pulse* of terror
      49 candles snuffed out
      Feel the *Pulse* of grief
53 lives hang in the balance
Feel the *Pulse* of hope
      Hundreds line up to donate blood
      Feel the *Pulse* of Orlando
            Vigils for the victims pop up everywhere
            Feel the *Pulse* of a Nation
                Our friends in Europe and Canada stand with us
            Feel the *Pulse* of the world
            We will not give in to fear and hatred
            Feel the *Pulse* of our Family
      We will reopen
      Feel the *Pulse* strengthen and continue
Remember the *Pulses* that beat no more
For they will live in our hearts forever

–Brian G Siebold

Life is short, so break the rules,
forgive quickly, kiss slowly, love
truly, laugh uncontrollably,
and NEVER regret anything
that made you smile.

~ UNKNOWN

Tonia Browne

TONIA BROWNE is an author, teacher and coach. As a teacher, Tonia has worked in the United Kingdom and internationally for over twenty years and was an Assistant Head for seven. She is a strong advocate of inviting fun into our lives and encouraging people to see their world from a different perspective.

Amazon Author's page:
Amazon.co.uk: http://www.amazon.co.uk/-/e/B00ZATHS4M
Amazon.com: http://www.amazon.com/Tonia-Browne/e/B00ZATHS4M
My Blog: time4tblog.wordpress.com
My Facebook page: Time4T @ facebook.com/Time4Tonia
My Twitter: twitter.com/ToniaUae

Coats and Wishes

Stars in Coats

"We are just stars that come into this world with a coat to wear and limitless wishes to make," he said. "Our mission is to wear the coat well, especially when the wind blows cold, and to use our wishes wisely."

His words were the words of wisdom delivered from a heart that now travels free from the restrictions of this mortal coil. His coat wore out but his wishes continue and his star still shines. It's the same for all of us I hope; eternal beings in an infinite universe.

Coats

He was born with great ceremony to a family in London. They wore their coats and made their wishes and they had many expectations for their firstborn son. "Be happy!" said one who had travelled and experienced much. "Make something of your life," said the other who had aspirations for her son that went beyond what she had achieved in her own life.

As for my father, "I was born in 1931 on 4th April at two o'clock in the morning and although I must have been there at the time, I remember nothing of that event at all," he commented with his usual wit. Yet, on the whole, he realised his parents' wishes for he smiled often and achieved much.

I have so many memories of my father. Some include his dedication and focus in helping me to learn. He would never give up trying to find different ways to support me. I remember him cutting out cardboard arrows to represent the wind and making model windsurfers out of lollypop sticks to demonstrate where to put the sail when the wind blew from different directions. I remember hours of chemistry instruction and even more hours spent with him showing me how to use his computer, a skill and a hobby he delighted in during his later life. He was also my master editor. Happy to dedicate hours to hone my writing skills. He gave the same dedication whether it was for a speech, for a work report or a message to a family member across the seas.

He had a varied life, some by choice and some by chance. His career took him to many lands and life took him to many careers. This meant he was not always physically with us at times, but we always knew he was there for us.

My sister summed his life up beautifully in a poem she wrote soon after his death in an attempt to understand the passing of a life from physical form.

My Father

My father—a strong and reassuring presence throughout my life.
Not always here, but always there ...

A young man with fair hair in a blue uniform with shiny buttons.
With fast cars and noisy planes,
And blue skies without rain.
Not always here, but always there ...

Older now, but in his prime,
With sand and sea and laughter and wine.
Large cars and colourful sails, diving masks and Arabian tales.
Not always here, but always there ...

An old man now, but forever young,
With BBQs and computers and sun.
Glass in hand, book in lap, always ready with advice on tap.
Not always here, but always there ...

The chair is now empty and the man has now gone.
The days are much quieter but the laughter lives on.

My father—a strong and reassuring presence throughout my life.
No longer here—but always there ...

~ Donnelly, N. My Father, unpublished, 2012

Wishes

It was his wish to leave something to this world. He mentioned his pride for his family and how at times he could not believe that he, with a bit of help, had created two amazing girls! "I am not a religious man," he would say, "but I believe in kindness."

He left his body to medical science. "Don't forget that, will you?" he said. "They may not want it by the time I have finished with it. But, if they do, it will be good to know that it can go on and help others who need theirs a little longer. I was a teacher in life and maybe I can be one in death too," he said.

He got his wish and by a strange series of events, his body returned to the area of his family's hometown.

Many were appalled when they heard what was to become of his body. They would prefer it to be honoured with reverence in accordance to their traditions and ceremonies. "Give the respect to the living," he always said. "But while living, remember to achieve your dreams and continue to make your wishes!"

He achieved much in his life. He wrote about many of those experiences in his unpublished memoirs. Towards the end of his memoirs he included a list, parts of which I have included here:

Achievements

So what have I done that I am especially pleased with?
Well, in no particular order, as they say, here goes:
- I have been married to the same lady for over fifty years and we still get on more or less OK.
- I have produced a pair of perfectly lovely children, been able to give them a good education and watched them go on to lead lives to be proud of.
- I am the grandfather of delightful twins.
- I have flown an aeroplane at more than twice the speed of sound.
- I have ridden a motorcycle at over 150 mph.
- I have paddled a dugout canoe across a lake in Borneo.
- I have taught many people to do things better than I could ever do them myself.
- I have ridden an Arab stallion bareback across the sands of Arabia, as my father did many years earlier.
- I have built three boats, one of which was exhibited at The Wooden Boat Show at Greenwich.

- I have SCUBA dived in wrecks and with sharks.
- I have sailed a windsurfer at over 30 knots.
- At the age of 59, I came ninth out of over 120 in a series of windsurfing races.
- I have played ice hockey and jumped over barrels on a frozen lake.
- I had the helm of a big sailing boat, at night, in a force eight gale, from Brightling Sea to Ostend.
- I have enjoyed almost everything I have done in my life!

Thank you everyone.

~ From: Browne, R. D. All About Grandad: Pearls of Wisdom, unpublished and incomplete, 2012

Stars

As I was concluding this chapter with tears in my eyes, remembering a life well lived, my gaze was diverted by a sign flashing on my computer screen signaling a new Facebook post; "Wayne Dyer is dead." I stopped typing this chapter and searched the internet for more. I found this:

Wayne has left his body, passing away through the night. He always said he couldn't wait for this next adventure to begin and had no fear of dying. Our hearts are broken, but we smile to think of how much our scurvy elephant will enjoy the other side.
We Love You Forever Dad/Wayne.
~ The Dyer Family: Facebook: 31 August 2015

My eyes then saw another post:

I have a suit in my closet with the pocket cut out. It's a reminder to me that I won't be taking anything with me. The last I wear won't need any pockets.
~ Dr. Wayne Dyer: Facebook: 28 August 2015

I returned to my chapter feeling emotional but clear. I knew that there was an additional message to add.

These incredible individuals with their gentle, hypnotic voices came to this planet and told their stories and shared their wisdom. Although they are no longer here, they will always be there. It is now our time to stand tall and continue to tell their stories and our own. It is time to be brave and to share their words ourselves. But more than this now — it is time to live in their wisdom and believe in their words.

Indeed, we are all amazing stars in coats; coats with wishes. How will you wear yours and how many wishes will you realise? This is the wisdom that is passed down through eternal stars wearing borrowed coats. This is the wisdom shared from wild hearts travelling in the skies as stars and guiding lights.

For the light and the essence of my father and all those that went before and will come after, may we continue to shine for them as they do for us.

Thank you to my mum and dad for always being there, for my friends and family who held my hand as we danced through life and to my amazing sister who is here with me throughout it all. A thank you to the fabulous Lisa and her VIP team who have been amazing to work with, and to my fantastic husband, who gave me confidence and space to write.

Dedicated to my father and to all our shining lights. May they continue to motivate us. Also dedicated to all those who believed in me. To my family, to my friends and the lovely people I have met and I have yet to meet. To you if you are reading this today and for those who will read it tomorrow—thank you and all the best.

~ Tonia Browne

Carole Cassell

CAROLE CASSELL is a licensed Heal Your Life® Coach, Workshop Leader, Law of Attraction Coach, Assertiveness Coach, author and speaker.

Carole spent many years questing to understand the deeper meaning in her life experiences. Along the way she acquired countless tools and techniques that allowed her to heal from her painful past, follow her dreams and design a life she loves.

Carole is passionate about sharing those tools of transformation to help others reconnect with their inner wisdom, find the gifts in their life experiences, heal from past wounds and design a life rich in love, happiness, inner peace, confidence and abundance.

Her greatest joy is spending time with her amazing sons, D.J. and Zach, and incredible husband, Roger. She also enjoys relaxing on the beach, hiking, traveling and spending time with her friends.

www.carolecassell.com

Weighted Down

"When are you due?" asked the smiling stranger standing behind me in the line at a public restroom. She glided her hand ever-so-gently over my extended tummy.

"I'm not sure," I replied, barely able to make eye contact. Luckily a stall became available and I didn't have to figure out what to say next. The previous occupant was narrowly out of the way before I dashed in, latched the lock, fell back against the cold metal door and wept.

You see, the thing is, I wasn't pregnant … I was overweight.

This event set in motion a battle with my weight that developed into a crippling experience that impacted my life for many years and in many ways.

I'd always been thin growing up. In fact, I'd been teased throughout school because of it. The other kids called me names like "Skinny Minnie," "Beanpole," and "String Bean." It never really bothered me. I was what I was and I was fine with that. Even after the birth of my two children, I quickly bounced back to my slender body. I ate what I wanted (within reason), exercised several times a week and that was pretty much the extent of my thoughts around weight. That is, until my early forties when I began taking steps towards my dream life.

When I met my husband, Roger, I was at my ideal weight. But during our first couple of years of dating, I gained 10 pounds. We joked it was my "happy weight" as my pre-Roger life was filled with stress, bouts of extreme depression and lots of anger. I'm not suggesting that upon marrying Roger those emotions vanished. Quite the opposite. They magnified.

However, there was something different about this relationship. I knew, deep down inside, this man showed up in my life to challenge all that I believed, to illuminate how I reacted to situations, and to support me in uncovering the true me — the "me" that lurked beneath the incredible pain and disappointment that had plagued me most of my life and was desperately longing to be free.

The same was true for him as well. We were the proverbial soulmates. Both incredibly supportive and encouraging of each other's growth. But even though we offered each other a safe place to heal, our journey of self-growth was not a smooth one. We endured a lot of pain and suffering in the name of growth. Everything we'd stuffed down and ignored over the years, floated to the surface for healing. And every bit of pain, insecurity and fear rose up and manifested in unexpected ways.

My deepest pain could be traced back to being told repeatedly by my father that I was a "worthless piece of shit" — despite successes I'd achieved in life that proved otherwise. And although I healed this deep-seated belief in the areas of relationships and my general health, as I began to step into the truth of who I was and serve others from my Higher Self, those old insecurities found a new way to stop me from shining. Crafty, little devils.

And what does this have to do with my weight?

Everything.

The Bully

Years ago, I received a call from the Divine to leave my corporate job as a controller and enter the world of the healing arts. I followed my calling to open a massage and bodywork practice and became successful very quickly. To compliment my business, I studied to be a life coach. I wanted to help people make peace with their pasts so they could be free to create a life they loved — just like I was doing. But it was also during this journey that I began to gain weight. Lots and lots of weight.

As I trained for the various licenses and certifications to assist clients in areas such as assertiveness, stress management, Law of Attraction and Louise Hay's "Heal Your Life," more of my own "stuff" came up for healing. I'd work on one thing, and then another would surface. I'd heal that, and then another would come up.

Being an overachiever by nature, I welcomed the awareness and opportunities for growth. I enjoyed the challenge of learning something new and then figuring out how to apply it to become an even better version of myself. And over the last seven years I healed childhood abuse, the pain and guilt from multiple failed marriages and family drama among other issues. If it came up, I healed it and moved on. My life was finally becoming the life I'd envisioned.

Except for one little thing... well... maybe not so little.

With each step I took to becoming more in alignment with my true essence, the bigger my goals and dreams became. The bigger my goals and dreams became, the bigger my dress size became. And as my weight climbed, I reacted the way I'd been taught to react.

I dieted.

I tried everything, but my weight wouldn't budge. And when dieting failed, I consulted my doctor. I knew there had to be something amiss in my body. He agreed; knowing weight had never been an issue for me before. But he couldn't find anything wrong and said I needed to face the fact that I came from a family with weight issues and should make peace with it.

He asked me a question, however, that stuck with me all these years later. He asked if I'd rather be fat and happy, or go back to the way my life once was, but be thin. Without hesitation I said I'd rather be fat and happy. Yet I wondered: *Why couldn't I be happy AND thin?*

My doctor suggested I watch what I eat, exercise regularly and see what happens. So I hired a nutritionist and a personal trainer and worked diligently. I ate exactly what they told me to eat, exercised precisely for how long and how often my trainer prescribed, and I lost nothing.

Nada. Zip. Zilch. My weight remained unchanged.

After a few months, I felt defeated. I called it quits and decided to make friends with my weight. After all, my husband still looked at me like I was the most beautiful woman in the world (thank you, Honey). And my family and friends didn't care how much I weighed. So for the next couple of years, I did my best to accept that I was simply a bigger woman. And that's when things got worse. I became my own personal bully. Each time I saw myself in a full-length mirror, I'd say the most horrific things to myself like:

Disgusting!

Look at you, you're no good for anything.

You're a fat pig.

You're an embarrassment.

You're a worthless piece of shit!

Yep, you read that last one right. I used the exact line on myself that my Dad used to say to me. I picked up right where he left off. Every time I saw my reflection, I'd stop and verbally abuse myself, taking care to point out all of the things that were wrong with me. I'd call myself names, names that I'd never dream of calling anyone else who looked like me:

Fatty.

Loser.

Heifer.

Ugly.

Worthless.

I made fun of myself on a regular basis, joking about my size when I was around other people. No one else said a word to me about my weight. I was doing all of this to myself. I bullied myself into tears day after day. I became a skilled tormenter, inflicting verbal beatings, slowly ripping away at my soul and dimming my own light.

By the time my "making friends with my body" experiment came to a close, I'd been so ruthless that I once again felt the worthlessness I'd felt most of my early life. Although I didn't realize it at the time, I'd found another way to feel "less than" and to keep myself down. All of the lovely healing I'd done felt like it was for naught. I'd lost my shine and let my weight define me. I became a hermit. I declined social invitations and stopped going to things like festivals, concerts, or the beach—all things I loved. I quit everything that once brought me joy because I was so uncomfortable in my own skin. It was a living hell—but a hell of my own design.

The Gift

I begged the Universe to help me figure out the root cause of my experience. I cried, begged, and then cried some more. I couldn't figure out what I was doing wrong. I'd done everything society tells you to do to lose weight—but ended up heavier than ever. Then, during my meditations, I began receiving messages that my weight was a gift from my body.

A gift? Are you kidding me? Seriously?

Although my mind rejected this theory, my Spirit recognized the truth. And after months of meditation, more messages from Spirit and many conversations with people I loved and trusted, I began to see the truth too, and applied the healing modalities I'd been trained in, upon my own body. I changed my mindset, repaired my abusive relationship with myself and practiced self-acceptance and unconditional love for my body.

And what I came to realize was that because I still had an underlying belief (albeit deeply buried), that I was worthless; each time I stepped into my power, my body added a layer of fat—that is, protection—to keep me safe. Protection against the pain and disappointment I was certain would follow any good I allowed into my life.

Diet and exercise alone was like rolling a boulder uphill. Until I healed the deeper issue and changed the focus of my thoughts, I would continue to "fight" the battle of the bulge. But once I accepted my body, showed it appreciation and changed my focus to what I wanted to create (instead of what I didn't), everything began to change.

This was the missing piece to my painful puzzle. *This* was the key to ending my pain and suffering. And *this* would help me heal the damage I caused my Soul.

Once I truly accepted my body's gift of excess weight, I could get on with the business of healing. Once I truly realized that the transformation needed to come from the inside out, not the outside in, I could use the beautiful tools I'd been trained in to change my reality and create the body I wanted. And once I truly released what society told me about weight loss, and began to listen to the wisdom from within, I became empowered.

And that's when my body began to lovingly release the excess weight.

Unconditional Love

Sometimes we're too close to a problem to really see what's going on. Sometimes we're so used to reacting in the way we've been conditioned, that we ignore our inner guidance that's screaming there must be another way, a better way.

Because I was so focused on changing my outer world—spending my time and energy dieting, exercising or beating myself up—I wasn't in the space to hear what my soul actually needed—kindness, acceptance and unconditional love.

I have since apologized to myself—body, mind and Spirit.

I now accept myself just as I am and that acceptance has created an environment for my body to return to its natural state of wellbeing.

And *now* when I pass a mirror, I stop and tell myself things like:

I love you!

You're so beautiful!

You're an amazing woman!

You deserve to have it all!

You are worthy!

I spend time each day in gratitude for my body and the way it was trying to protect me. I thank it for showing up for me 100 percent while it carried around 80 extra pounds and suffered the negative effects of yo-yo dieting, punishing workouts and verbal abuse.

I spend time each day feeding my Spirit with positive self-talk—loving words that honor me and highlight my worth.

And I spend time each day meditating and visualizing my future self, deeply connecting with the feeling of once again having my ideal body and the freedom of no longer feeling weighted down.

I'm both happy and excited that my body is releasing its excess weight naturally. No more diets, no more brutal workouts, just simple, healthy eating and exercise I enjoy.

And of course … the power of the mind.

Dedicated to those of you for whom the battle of the bulge has taken its toll on your soul—may my story empower you to practice unconditional self-love and to remind you that you are beautiful, amazing and worthy—just the way you are!

A huge, heartfelt thanks to my family and friends for your unwavering support and unconditional love. And to my husband Roger—thank you for always looking at me the way you did on our wedding day.

Special thanks to Debby, Dawn and Christine—the greatest friends in the world. Thank you for picking me up when I was down, reminding me of my gifts and for letting me see myself through your eyes. My love for you is beyond measure.

~ Carole Cassell

Lindsley Silagi

LINDSLEY SILAGI, is an educator and professional coach with a private coaching practice, *Step By Step Results!* located in Santa Teresa, New Mexico where she lives happily with her husband, Lon. She loves to hold healing and motivational retreats in the enchanting state she calls home. Lindsley loves dance, art, music, nature, little kids, hot springs, gardening, books, striking up a friendship, photography, and travel.

www.stepbystepresults.net

Imagine, Just Imagine It

The title of this book inspired me to contribute to it. Wisdom, wild, and from the heart. First, this book is about wisdom. We all have wisdom, that knowledge that you gain from the experiences you have in life. Yet many times people do not value it or recognize how special it is. It is my hope that by reading the next few pages you will recognize your own wisdom more deeply and connect with who you really are. Next this book is about the "wild heart". Wild can mean untamed, unruly or out of control. According to the Merriam Webster online dictionary, wild can also mean "in a natural state or environment". This latter definition is the one that I am using and I would like you to think about. When wild is describing the heart in this way we can think of it as being a heart in a natural state. How do we bring our heart to its natural state? There are many practices, routines, and rituals that support us. You undoubtedly already know many of them: meditation, good sleep, eating well, connecting with others, having a regular spiritual practice. We can bring our hearts to a natural state over and over again by practicing a few of these to keep ourselves balanced and to keep our sense of well-being.

So combining these two, collected knowledge from my experience, and from a natural place within the heart, my message is simple: **Imagination Is Essential**.

This precept has served me well in life. So let's dig in together to uncover how I use the power of imagination and how it has served me in my life.

As a young girl growing up in Connecticut, I had the ideal time and space for developing my imagination. My childhood home was surrounded by acres of woodlands. I spent many hours exploring these woods. There were three huge boulders, (known as glacial erratics in geological terms), that beckoned me to climb them. These three boulders were each about 12 feet to 15 feet in height and 15 to 20 feet long. I would start a climb by getting a foothold of a crevice just big enough to place my foot and then reach out for a branch or vine to hoist myself upward. This was a challenging process and one with many slips and near catastrophic falls. But step-by-step I would usually get to the top of one of the boulders, my childhood playground for the afternoon. There I imagined myself as explorer, conqueror, and Queen of the Forest. It was a truly enchanting place and time. I would richly imagine the top surface of the boulder as my own. It was big enough to walk upon, with mosses, lichen, and fairy bells flowering upon it. I would sit upon a section of that boulder in a special place that was like a throne. There I would smile upon the land that was all mine. It was through these experiences over time that I learned an appreciation of nature, confidence in self, a strong sense of direction, and self-determination. These were the attributes that I acquired through the development and use of my imagination.

While I loved my home and the woods surrounding them so much early on in life, I also imagined a life where you could see the sky. Yes, for all of the beauty of the forest lands, I longed to see for miles around. I dreamed of a place where sunrises and sunsets filled the wide expansive sky. I used to write story after story and draw landscapes of a place where there were open skies, a place where you could see forever. Later in my life this imagined place came to be in my real life, a life I live today under the richly beautiful and ever enchanting New Mexico skies.

As a young girl I also imagined my future self and what I wanted to do in life. Step-by-step, on my path to achieve this image, it developed in rich detail. By the time I was seven I knew I wanted to be a teacher. I imagined this and practiced it in child's play with friends and neighbors. My friends and I would gather at my home where we would take turns delivering instruction and assigning lessons to one another. During my high school years, I tutored young students in the elementary school. The classroom teacher would give me the most challenging students to reach. I loved those early challenges and the feeling I got as I helped them to succeed. When I graduated, I said yes to an opportunity to teach preschool. It was in Chicago. I moved there for a year prior to beginning my formal college studies. These early experiences fueled my imagination for the future teaching experiences I would have when my studies were complete.

Time and time again from living life in Chicago, Vermont and then to the desert southwest, it has been the use of the power of imagination that has helped me attain my next best version of myself. After teaching children for many years, I jumped at the opportunity to teach teachers the successful strategies that I had learned and used in my classroom. These included literacy strategies, mathematics strategies and the incorporation of technology. Next I transitioned into leading district level change initiatives. After that I started supporting educational improvement efforts by finding funding for those important efforts, which I still do today. I believe that it was the time that I spent alone, using my imagination that helped me form strong images of who I was and who I could become. What I recognize today is that as I turn to alone time, I am better able to connect to who I am and who I am becoming. I am able to bring a picture of what I want to do and what it will look like. I imagine it richly. I see it happening in my mind's eye first.

It was imagination that helped my husband and I as we became ready to buy our first home. The first house that we ever owned was one that I dreamt about first. I imagined the neighborhood in detail and I imagined the house vividly too. I imagined us living in a neighborhood complete with a community pool and tennis courts. I imagined a home with a mountain view. And then one day not long after I started imagining this dream home, I saw a tiny advertisement no bigger than a half inch describing a home for sale. I called the number listed and made an appointment on the spot. Two days later my husband and I saw the house and knew it was perfect for us the moment we arrived. The neighborhood as well was all that I envisioned. Our purchase of that house moved along quite fluidly and without obstacles in the details. Friends and family were amazed that within a week we were in our new home! Imagination was clearly one of the powers at work. I credit imagination to the manifestation of that home and the swift move into it.

The purchase of our second home also happened almost as effortlessly. We viewed that house on our way to get the groceries for the week and by the time we had the groceries in our car, we knew we would call the real estate agent with an offer. Looking back upon that time it was the imagining that came before the purchase that made the actual transaction swift and simple.

Professionally, in every presentation that I have given, and in every project I have developed, imagination has been involved. But I want to make an important point here. I cannot say that I was intentionally using my imagination for getting richly desired results. It was not that I wanted bigger, better, or best. It was simply that my imagination was always at work. Now looking back upon my life, I see that it was the power of imagination at work that helped propel me from one success to another. And so it is now, that I have a deeper appreciation for it.

I share my experience with you so you can see how it can empower your life. No matter what your dreams are, you can do it. Imagination will help you get there. So develop it. Use it actively as the tool it is. Step-by-step you can imagine what it is you want to do, whether a short term project or a lifelong ambition. But you must quiet your mind. You must be still and peaceful within yourself as you do imagine the future you want to create. Stay true to the use of your imagination and you will find that you are able to see your dreams come true. Taking time for the quiet needed to imagine yourself and what is possible is essential to your future success.

If you want to change how your life is unfolding, a great way to begin is to imagine what is possible for you. In your mind's eye, see all of the details unfolding the way you want them to unfold. You can do this. Stay true to the use of your imagination. It is a powerful way to shape your life. It is on your side, empowering you to be the best you can be.

To Lon, my husband and my best friend, who makes me smile every day of the week.

Thank you to all who have touched my life. You do know who you are. And because of you I know myself more fully.

~Lindsley Silagi

Lisa Hardwick

Many believe that they were blessed when the Universe led them directly to LISA HARDWICK to assist them with the roadmap to living their life's purpose. Lisa is fiercely committed to guiding Spiritual Entrepreneurs to achieve their dream of becoming a published author, to help them build a strong network and to assist them with a plan that works so they can make an abundant living doing what they are passionate about.

If you're looking for a proven professional who can guide you to Develop an Action Plan of everything you will need to succeed and create financial energy as a Spiritual Entrepreneur, then you've come to the right place.

With many years of experience working with clients and guiding them to achieve remarkable success, her mission is to share valuable tools and resources so you can make an actual living as a Spiritual Entrepreneur. If you're ready to answer the call and align with your passion by taking the simple steps to make it your life's work, then connect with her today to set up an initial consultation.

To learn more about Lisa, please visit: www.lisahardwick.com.

🦋 Aunt Ruthie's Wild Heart

I sat at my desk; pen in hand, agonizing over what to write about for this book. I had many ideas in mind for the theme—wisdom from the wild heart—yet one idea continued to beckon me. It was as if it kept raising its hand saying, "Pick me! Pick me!" That particular idea related to my Great Aunt Ruthie.

My late aunt's name came up just a few weeks prior when a friend asked me about my upcoming milestone birthday—the BIG 5-0. I told her I was actually looking forward to it. That it seemed the older I got, the more comfortable I felt in my own skin, the wiser I became and the more I enjoyed celebrating my unique self. I told her I was feeling more like my Great Aunt Ruthie, who was a kindred spirit and definitely wild at heart.

Aunt Ruthie never had any children of her own so she gave a lot of attention to her nieces and nephews. She was adorably quirky, and loved by everyone who knew her. She wrote funny poems and sang silly songs and shared side-splitting jokes. Well...they really weren't *that* funny...but to me, that's what made them hilarious.

She had her own style and was comfortable being herself—her funky, creative, awesome self. And as I looked back, I realized she was different than anyone else I knew, or would ever know. I laughed out loud just thinking about how *cool* that woman actually was—even at her age!

I'll never forget the time Aunt Ruthie joined my family for Thanksgiving dinner in the late '90s. In the middle of the meal, she pushed aside her plate and dug around in her purse with a determined look on her face. She smiled broadly as she pulled out a big yellow envelope containing some pictures she had just gotten developed.

Aunt Ruthie flipped slowly through the pictures. Once finished, she passed the large stack to the person sitting beside her, who looked at them before passing them onto the next person and so on, until they eventually got to me.

The photos were from a Halloween party Aunt Ruthie had recently attended. There were lots of images of her friends dressed up in the traditional Halloween costumes—ghosts, witches, Dracula, Frankenstein. There was even a couple dressed as Raggedy Ann and Andy.

When I got to the picture of Aunt Ruthie I hooted with laughter. She was wearing a miniskirt with a flamboyant top along with a lot of jewelry. On her feet she wore a pair of bright white knee-high boots.

"Were you a go-go dancer, Aunt Ruthie?" I asked.

She flipped her hair and said matter-of-factly, "I was Scary Spice from the Spice Girls." Then she winked at me.

My brother was sitting next to me at the table. We turned and looked at each other with big eyes. The two of us laughed with such joy at how young-at-heart and hip our much-loved aunt was to dress up as someone from this popular '90s girl band. Aunt Ruthie always made everyone feel good when she was around and she was an absolute gift in my life.

As I shared the story with my friend, I vowed to be just like Aunt Ruthie when I was in my 70s. I affirmed to never lose my spunk, my creativeness, my quirkiness, and especially my sense of humor. I wanted people to feel just as good around me, as we did around Aunt Ruthie. I wanted to be just as wild at heart at 50 as she was at 70.

Still wavering as to what to write about, I pushed aside the idea along with my intuition. I logged into my computer to see if there might be some kind of sign as to what I should share. As my computer came out of sleep-mode, I noticed my Facebook page was onscreen. I didn't remember being on Facebook and wondered how that happened.

Knowing how distracting social media could be, especially for a writer, I decided to sign out...yet a post caught my eye. It was by an old friend whom I hadn't connected with in a very long time. I felt guided to visit her profile page. I scrolled through one of her first posts—it was an article about the Spice Girls!

If that wasn't a clear sign, I don't know what else would have been. Aunt Ruthie was determined that I write about her.

And what a great reminder, I thought, to always follow that soft, loving whisper that nudges you to take action—whether to make a call, drive down a certain road, or turn your computer on—because every time I've listened and followed that voice, it's led me to incredible places, ideas and people.

Seems like Aunt Ruthie was still having her fun. And still very much in my life.

A few days later I was still thinking about my aunt. Once again I felt a sense of something deep inside. I had a whisper, a "knowing," that I was supposed to see something, or hear something, yet I wasn't quite sure what I needed to do for whatever it was to reveal itself to me. I felt moved to meditate to see what might come up. Perhaps then the answer would be revealed.

I positioned myself in my favorite meditative pose and focused on some soothing music. I relaxed enough to tap into the Divine. I patiently listened for the whispers of my soul.

Finally, it came—I needed to acknowledge my disappointment and frustration of not having the opportunity to say goodbye to my dear aunt so I could heal my heart. I still missed her after all these years.

I felt the pain of the story bubbling up from deep within. I recalled the day I learned of her passing. It was 2002. I was driving. I remembered the phone call, yet I couldn't remember if it was summer or winter. I couldn't remember if I was on my way to work, or coming home when I received it. All I remembered was answering the call and my mother saying that she had gone to a service for Ruth the day before.

"Ruth?" I asked. "Ruth who?"

"Your Aunt Ruth," my mother replied.

I pulled the car over and sobbed for a long time. I was living in another city at the time so I hadn't seen the obituary. And everyone in my family thought that someone else had told me. I had no idea my beloved Aunt Ruthie had transitioned. My heart felt as if it had broken into a million little pieces.

I felt guided to connect with my aunt and let her know how much she meant to me, how much I loved her, and how sorry I was that I wasn't there with the family to celebrate her beautiful life. I shared my feelings with her Spirit. Happy tears fell as I experienced such relief.

I got up from my meditation feeling considerably lighter, joyful and balanced, just like I felt whenever I was in Aunt Ruthie's presence. To me, that was a sign that she had heard me.

I went to my computer and did a Google search for her obituary. I'd never read it before and felt drawn to read it. It took a while but I finally found it.

My eyes immediately zeroed in on my name in the middle of the article. I was listed as her great niece. I smiled thinking about how much I must have meant to her, too.

I then began to read the obituary, and as I read, I felt something—something very strong. I kept reading and the feeling got stronger. I stopped right in my tracks when I got to the fourth line which read, "Memorial service celebrating her life will be held at 7:00 p.m. on Monday, March 18, 2002."

March 18? It couldn't be!

I jumped up to look at the calendar on my desk. In my excitement, I dropped it on the floor. I picked it up and scrambled to find the day's date…

March 18, 2016.

I am honored to utilize this opportunity to acknowledge those who lovingly share my space with me each and every day, Great Aunt Ruthie, Grandma Peggy, Grandma Bonnie, Cousin Heather, Cousin Mandi, Great Aunt Barbara, and many others I hold dear to my heart. I am open to continue to receive your loving signs.

Dedicated to Taylor Benge, also a niece loved dearly by Great Aunt Ruthie. May this story assist you with feeling the loving presence of those who have transitioned to the next experience and help you with the 'knowing' that you are guided and supported by them on your own personal life path. Keep your eye out for ladybugs!

~Lisa Hardwick

Catherine Madeira

CATHERINE MADEIRA is a freelance writer and artist. She has been receiving ethereal information for years and is now sharing it in the hope of helping others in their life's journeys.

Catherine is from the Reno/Tahoe area and has two children, Jason, who has always demanded an intellectual approach to life, and daughter, Kendal, who was born a very old soul. Catherine has been documenting her experiences for years. Subsequently, she has been able to receive, evaluate, and compile the information to pass to others.

umbriel03@gmail.com

Do You Remember the Ships?

Aura Envisioned

Please my friend share with me
The light that only you can see
You say it shines from everyone
All places, everything
The way you see their beauty
Hidden deep inside
You say it shows on all of us
The radiance of life
It precedes us as we approach you
Trails behind us as we leave
The light of life and beauty in all
That only you can see

~Catherine Madeira

In this chapter let's discuss our dreams. I am not going to insult your intelligence by insinuating that you have not already questioned the mystery and significance of dreams. I know that any insightful person wonders about the dreaming and relationship to our daily lives. I am though, going to mention all kinds of different experiences in the dream state and let's see if you have had similar involvement and maybe we can start connecting the dots and find a place of oneness. Many of us wake and keep journals of our episodes, many of us often wake wishing we had written down one of the events we had the previous night. But then the night visions slip away from us so quickly and we forget our participation. I often have grand adventures in my sleep and in a matter of moments of waking the happenings are again hidden from me.

Why I wonder in our dreams, are we interacting with and know very well, people whom in this life we have never met. But in the scape they are trusted friends and mutual travelers. I question if I am having shared encounters with other humans. Do we slide into certain and separate dimensions and actually interact with each other? But because we are, in general, not spiritually connected on this planet we are unaware that we are in fact relating in the space? Is it possible that on other planets with civilizations' who are not as spiritually conflicted as we are, that their dream state is a conscious connection between comrades, roamers and they recognize the reality of the relative condition?

Also, there are the separate categories and types of dreams, and as mentioned above some are interactive adventures with unknown friends. But other actions direct us to our premonition realm. I do not believe the premonition zones are the interactive. Those are the serious areas we are drawn to in which we are tasked to witness an event and are compelled to share said event often to our own detriment. We have already discussed this in previous books, *Whispers of the Heart* and *The Empowerment Manual*. *The Empowerment Manual*, chapter titled *Adjustable Foresight*, describes the premonitory experience of it fully, so we won't stray again too far into this region as it has already been discussed.

Probably the most lifting and important manifestation is when we are visited by passed loved ones. I personally do not believe these fall into our list of categories. I am convinced that those interactions with our passed family and friends are real, tangible meetings from the different planes. These are a gift driven by Love. This is happening in the REM zones but doesn't apply to our examination of interacting with beings we don't consciously know. Never the less, have you had visitation from loved ones who have passed away?

I believe the dream zones range so vastly in category and purpose that we, as a budding civilization certainly can't count the zones, let alone identify and categorize them. We have the dreams where we know we are on station and have a hand in controlling the course and outcome of what is happening in said experience. Those can be fun.

Let's explore a couple other possible common aspects. While in the realm of REM sleep.

You can't run or swing your arms. We can't lift our eyes and or see anything but a small slit on the ground ahead of us while being perused or having to get someplace. I sometimes end up underwater, since I cannot drown while sleeping I discover that I can tentatively breathe, those can be interesting as well. There are many ventures that take us places that are familiar in the dream that we have never been to physically.

Though I live in an arid region, I often find myself swimming, on a boat, or next to the ocean. I had a dream or a memory that I was in space, I was with other people, really profound. Do you have related transports and challenges, do any of these spontaneous activities seem familiar to you? Do you dream you are with trusted friends that in the waking state you do not know? I think this leads us to something larger than we are currently aware of. I recently had a REM action, in which I was a completely different person, I was a woman but I wasn't me, I was taller than I am, I had different legs and feet, I was wearing a brown pencil skirt with peplum style jacket and I was simply walking through some type of very old style housing or apartment project, I was on a second or third floor, the halls were not as wide as they are in newer style housing. There was lots of stylized Iron railing. The floors were a worn white tile material. I felt as though I may have been in France or someplace like that. I had a small male child with me and we were simply making our way through these rooms looking for someone or something. Now that could have been another memory of me in another life, similar to what we discussed in the book, *Awaken*. Or did I somehow join with a living person and piggy back them for a short time? Whatever that was it was in the realm of the real. If I was meshing with a woman, then that was a first for me as far as I know. If that is the case, then I did not know that the living could network with the living. I have heard of spontaneous joining of certain types of clairvoyant but the possibility of a living person merging momentarily with another living had never occurred to me as being possible. Probably something we should eventually return to and discuss further.

Switching directions, we have all heard the old wives' tale that if you fall from great heights in dreams and hit the ground, you do not wake in the physical form. I can attest that you do in fact wake up. I know because I often fall in my excursions and I hit the ground each and every time. I wake at the end of the dream. I have had it happen so many times now that I just get up and continue on with the adventure.

Then we have our levitation dreams, the levitation intrigues me. The flying occasions are different. I have wondered before if the levitation interest me because I may actually be lifting off the sleep location a little bit. How would I know if I am or not, there is no one there to see? But in the levitation experience it is always in the location I currently am, I never lift up much, just enough to make it seem real and then I wake up. So am I spontaneously actually lifting?

The flying offers glimpses of freedom for those of who have the good fortune of that action. They occur in all different places and we move through the dream landscape. When you fly, do you fly alone or with others? Some people just jump great distances. Others have super strength. Do any of these previous mentions relate to you?

A little personal note about me, I live this life without the gift of having found my soulmate. I know I have one but I do not feel his or its presence in this world. So other than family and very few friends, I live my life without an intimate companion and love of my life. But I have had a couple (only a couple) of dreams in which that missing soulmate has joined me. In these moments the connection with this individual is so moving and profound its astonishing how secure and complete I felt when I am joined by this individual. The presence filled the void. When I have been forced from those interdimensional connections I have been very upset and lonely upon the exit, and that loneliness affects me even now. Those of you who were granted the gift of sharing this life with your soulmate are indeed very fortunate. Going through this life void of the and having him come to me in those dreams must be accepted as that is all I am granted at this time. I am given the gift of knowing he is there and having the short experience with the individual, but the time is so fleeting. I have reluctantly accepted that he waits for me elsewhere and in another incarnation we will be joined again. We will continue on where we left off on our next adventure together. In this life my dictate is to try to inform others with as much information as I am able, so this is me trying to fulfill my duty.

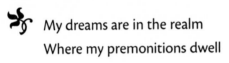 My dreams are in the realm
Where my premonitions dwell

~ CATHERINE MADEIRA

That little verse, is a small statement with a very large meaning. The title of this Chapter is *Do You Remember the Ships?* So the other type of dream I would like to ask you about is exactly that. Have you seen the ships and do you remember? In my dreams I see ships, Spaceships. I will openly admit I have experienced, during waking hours, several UFO sightings, as have my children. I will get further into the sightings in an upcoming chapter in one of the next publications but I will say I have seen UFOs from a distance of several miles and on one occasion much closer in broad daylight. I am sure you have also seen things like I have. All you really have to do is look up and watch for a while.

Returning to the spaceships in the dreams … I have seen, in dreams, enormous spaceships. From the ground looking up, these are enormous spaceships. They are partially transparent or cloaked but you can see them. In these scenes, I am not alone, these giant spaceships are visible to all and my fellow watchers are reacting to them. I was home in Reno, Nevada and these giant spaceships appeared. Some in the daylight and the others at night. To me they almost looked like glass or again masked or cloaked. The giant spaceships are accompanied by smaller spaceships maneuvering across the skyline and lingering around the giant spaceships. Other spaceships are not masked, but in motion and completely visible. I mention these because I am so moved in the dramatic events. This is exciting stuff when it's happening. They have more of the feel of reality. I ask you if you have ever seen the spaceships? We will never know if it's a shared reality unless we tell one another. So I am telling you I have seen them. I am asking you, have you seen them also? Do these visions have something to do with the sounds being heard around the world now?

When I was a teenager, and I was in a home in Washoe Valley near Lake Tahoe, I would swear I was dreaming but I remember getting up and looking out of the window to the south of the home and in a very close proximity to the home, one hundred yards or so, was a small UFO spaceship just hovering there. That (dream) had impact, as I never forgot it and how real it seemed. Is any of this sounding familiar to you?

Continuing on with the UFO section a little further. About 8 years ago I was sleeping and I was having a contact, a classic abduction. I was laying on my back on a table, there were three to four very tall beings working around me, the space was not well lit. They looked like typical greys but were much taller. I was not afraid as I was being treated very gently and I felt safe under their care. The being to my left standing next to my head was physically holding my wrists with his hand. He held me with my wrists crossing with one of his very large hands and leaned down over my face with his face. I remember telling myself that this wasn't a dream and to remember, remember, remember. So that one I 'm just not sure about. Was it real? I almost hope so, they seemed to be kind and intended no harm.

I am not the only one in my family with the abduction dream. My mother had a very interesting abduction alternate reality 20 years ago in which she and my daughter, age eight, were abducted together. She remembers dreaming, being in the car with my daughter and all the vehicles around her in addition to her car stopped. All the street lights went out. Then she felt herself losing consciousness and put her arm over my daughter and she fell away to oblivion. The aspect of this (dream) that my mother, Lilas Hardin, found so unusual was that she was dreaming and then lost consciousness while dreaming. I personally think they were both abducted. Neither my mother nor my daughter Kendal ever exhibited any memory or negative effects from the occurrence. My daughter Kendal has no recollection of this at all. My son Jason has also had some quite profound notifications, but again all of those things we will explore in chapters to come.

In order for us as humans to help ourselves evolve to the level where there is possibility, we are going to have to risk the onset of ridicule and humiliation. We must decide to communicate with each other these things that are not commonly spoken of and step outside our comfort zone. We could be interacting with each other and never know it because we don't speak it. Our species, with few exceptions, has stalled. There is currently too much chaos and frankly too much mindless cruelty flowing unchecked through civilization on this planet. We are distracted with intentional nonsense that keeps drawing us away from the path of enlightenment. I am certain I am not telling you anything you are not already aware of. What I am attempting is to invite us toward one another so we can share and discover that we are having common connections.

Sharing

As the array of this life's experience unroll before our stride
We are drawn to focus on our own oncoming path
Instead we should observe the forward motion of our brethren in their roads' endeavors'
In watching the lanes adjacent to us we more fluently move forward together
We may evolve with more ease
As united our road to the Light is wider stronger and more predictable

~ Catherine Madeira

To summarize, we use the term, "dream" for a myriad of different states of consciousness that should probably have separate titles but don't thus far. We have the realm of visitations from loved ones and soulmates. Separate from that, the zones of premonitions or another departure, would be the abduction. Now adding to our list, are the unrealized contacts with the living and locations that do exist but that we don't know while we are awake. Each arena is being incorrectly categorized as the *dream state*. Visualizing all of the above as being a very relevant part of our lives will help expand and lift our frequency, pulling us closer to realization and togetherness. Do we interact with whole communities of people and beings and choose to forget it day after day? Let's begin focusing on breaking down that barrier. I feel, as a civilization, we could be much farther along than we are. For instance, our technology has surpassed our spirituality. It's thrown us off kilter. Most humans are not approaching the world from the origin of good intention. We cannot utilize "high-tech" or "god-tech" without the spiritual aspect in place, the puzzle cannot come together without both.

We are scripted to be good stewards of this planet. Evolve and then move to new planets and realms. We as representatives of Earth/Gaia will not be allowed to move forth until we have balanced the equation, only then may we venture on. Sharing the hidden spaces of our lives may prove to us that we are interacting and in turn, draw us closer to each other and assist us in rising to our intended potential.

Dedicated to my Granddaughter, Harlo Monroe, who we now believe is an Indigo. To my two tiny dogs, Bell, my best friend and angel on Earth, and Bee, Bell's lively assistant. My Father, Richard Madeira, who passed years ago but has stayed to watch over his family.

Lisa Hardwick the Publisher of Visionary Insight Press, for giving me the opportunity to share my information. Without this wonderful & accepting person I may have lived my life without being able to complete my purpose for coming here. I want to thank my mother, Lilas Hardin, for her support, my son, Jason Vaughan, and daughter, Kendal Vaughan, for always being available to discuss these complex matters. To my granddaughter, Harlo Monroe, as her existence alone motivates me to share my knowledge.

Thank you Lisa Hardwick, Publisher and Katina Gillespie, Managing Project Director, for editing my work and making it presentable.

~ Catherine Madeira

Cheryl Guttenberg

CHERYL GUTTENBERG is a licensed Heal Your Life® Coach and workshop leader, healer, author and speaker. As a Human Resources professional, Cheryl likes to join organizations and make them an even better place for the employees. She does this through her coaching and counseling and corporate technical skills.

Cheryl also assists individuals to find more peace and joy through her workshops and coaching practice.

Living in Southern California, Cheryl enjoys spending time with her family, travelling and ballroom, swing and Latin dancing as often as possible.

www.CherylGuttenberg.com
CherylGuttenberg@gmail.com

Next Chapter

My Perfect Job

For the past two years, I've been leading a team of human resources professionals for a family owned insurance company. With seven of us in the department, we provided immediate and personalized assistance to all our 250 employees. This was such a great place to work with a good compensation and benefit package and enabled me to utilize my prior 20 years of human resources management experience. I was able to make changes and guide the department and operational systems into the 21st century of human resources protocols.

I felt so grateful to have found such a wonderful position. I had landed my perfect position until I decided to retire. It would be another 5–7 years before I would transition to full time workshop leader and life coach.

Roller Coaster Ride

One Monday in early January, my boss Bob called and asked for a brief meeting. When I got off the phone, I remember thinking this was the first time he hadn't mentioned the reason for our meeting, Oh well, it's probably nothing important, I thought. When I arrived in Bob's office, I sat in the chair opposite his big cherry wood desk, with the large cabinet behind him displaying his family pictures and many books. Bob has never been a very expressive man. You never really knew what he was thinking. However, this morning I noticed something different. Bob had an enormous smile as he said, "I have some really exciting news.... the company has been bought by a large publicly held company." As I sat there with my poker face I responded, "Wow Bob, that is exciting news for you and your family." As I am thinking, well what in the heck will happen to the rest of us??? Bob continued to tell me I needed to keep the news confidential until the contract was signed. He listed the documents I would need to provide him for the due diligence process. I left Bob's office in a mental haze. I felt like I was just blind-folded and stepped onto a five story roller coaster without being able to see the track in front of me. Dozens of questions raced through my mind. What will happen to my position? What does this mean to my department? Who is this company? When will this happen?

That night after work, I called upon the people in my support system. They listened to me as I expressed tears, my fears, and anger. How could this be happening now? I was so set in my perfect position. This could potentially throw my job and finances upside down! Ultimately, my decision had been to turn it over to the Universe and let it go. This was not easy, as my first instinct was to panic! It was also important for me to reach out professionally and see if there were any other job opportunities. As a single woman, I need to be able to support myself. I needed a job!

 You cannot always control what goes on outside.

But you can always control what goes on inside.

~ DR. WAYNE DYER

Bumpy Road

By the end of January, the contract had been signed and all the employees were notified. The employees walked around in shock about the news. Everyone believed the company would have been handed down through the generations. This made perfect sense since there were three generations of family members currently working there.

A majority of our workforce had an average tenure of 20 plus years and not very accepting of change. For the following weeks, many employees walked around as though they were sleep walking.

Over the next few months, we went through the transition process. The new company's human resources team came out and held meetings with all the employees regarding the benefits and the company's policies and procedures. The new company with 5000+ employees was so much larger than our employee population. Our employees were used to a culture more generous and less structured than the new organization. There were few, if any, employees who were happy about the acquisition. Since I don't believe in coincidences, I found it fascinating I was going through this experience on a personal level, along with having to coach other employees dealing with the identical, huge change.

I had a conversation with the Vice President of Human Resources of the new company regarding my position. Since she and I had the same title, I knew that wouldn't work. She assured me that she saw a role for me as a director of the Western Region. I felt a little better but still had a somewhat uneasy feeling about it.

Yet again, I was realizing that life is not static, everything changes and the Universe always takes care of me. It was all the uncertainty which felt so unsettling. I'm a planner and like to know what's ahead of me ... Life has a way of showing up and offering us opportunities to take us out of our comfort zone.

 I have learned there is no need for me to struggle.

I trust the Universe to take care of me.

~ LOUISE HAY

As the acquisition date approached, more discontentment and non-productivity were evident across the organization. I continued to meet individually with many employees who wanted to discuss their options. One of the employees was a single Mom and had worked there for 20 years. After much discussion, she decided she would take the severance package. It was more frightening for her to stay with the new company. In the end, she saw it as an opportunity to broaden her career. There were other employees who sat in my office and just sobbed, feeling their professional lives were doomed. I listened with empathy and offered suggestions for consideration to aide in their decisions. Several employees were paralyzed in their fears and were resistant of this massive change in their lives.

The week before the close of the transaction, we learned 61 employees decided to take the severance package. So in our department, we prepared the severance packages along with the final paychecks and met with the employees to explain the off-boarding process. The employees were angry and afraid of the road ahead. The human resources department was left with just two of us. For me the decision was clear, I'm not ready to retire, so I would transition over to the new organization.

The next week it was over ... Those of us who stayed on continued with the new company, the only thing that remained familiar was we drove to the same worksite. Everything else was different, new bosses, processes, benefit plans, pay dates, and all dissimilar procedures.

Phew, we made it through to the other side ... This journey had some severe bumps in the process. It has been almost two months since the acquisition became effective. All of us continue to learn the re-definition of our work roles.

I learned more about myself during this process. A large lesson was I'm not the CEO of the Universe, so I couldn't fix everyone's problems during this time. I was thankful I could help by being a good listener, while employees worked through their decisions.

Next Chapter

This week my new boss came for a visit. She sent me an email last week stating she was coming out and wanted to meet individually with myself and my co-worker. I immediately got a sinking feeling in the pit of my stomach. My co-worker tried to reassure me she was probably just coming to visit to see how we are doing post acquisition. I let go my negative thoughts and feelings and proceeded to have a good weekend. My boss arrived on Wednesday and we met in my office. She explained to me that she could no longer justify my director position with the low employee count at our location. My job will be eliminated in September. I felt as though I was just slugged in the stomach.

 Some changes look negative on the surface, but you will soon realize that space is being created in your life for something new to emerge.

~ ECKHART TOLLE

I wonder what I will learn about myself with this next chapter. What I know for sure is I have to trust the Universe again on this one!!!

Bryon Katie teaches us "Loving What Is." I can't say I always love what is happening or even like what's occurring but I'm learning more about acceptance ... I find this to be best for my body, mind and spirit.

 Life is a series of natural and spontaneous changes. Don't resist them; that only creates sorrow! Let reality be reality. Let things flow naturally forward in whatever way they like.

~ LAO LZU

Dedicated to my self-appointed big sister, Maria Snyder. Over the past two decades, you have been my best friend, therapist, awesome cooking teacher and wise earth angel. For many years you have guided me through all my challenges and have always had the exact words I needed to hear, along with your loving support.

I have much gratitude for my spiritual teachers: Louise Hay, Dr. Wayne Dyer, Marianne Williamson, Cheryl Richardson, Dr. Patricia Crane and Rick Nichols. You all have opened my world to have no limits, and for that I am forever grateful.

~ Cheryl Guttenberg

D.J. Lawson

DJ LAWSON is a licensed Massage Therapist and practical Life Coach. After many years in management, DJ left his position to pursue a career in the healing arts. Little did he know that would be the beginning of his spiritual journey.

Over the last several years DJ overcame a major health scare by finding new ways to handle the stresses of day to day life. He loves to challenge the status quo, examine things from all angles and use that information to create a life on his terms.

DJ has an innate gift of connecting with people on a deep level, building trust and forming quality relationships with everyone he encounters. His diverse work history and many challenging life experiences have given him a very special set of skills to develop friendships and assist people on their healing journey.

www.djlawson.com

In A Box Without Walls

As I open my eyes, I see faces staring back at me. None of them are familiar. Their mouths move, speaking to me without sound. I feel no emotion at all and whatever's weighing me down is also preventing me from comprehending what's happening. I lie there—a prisoner in my own body.

I scan the area around me. It's small. I realize that I'm lying on my back and the faces in front me are actually looking down on me. I am unable to move or speak. After what feels like an eternity, my ears fill with sound. Slowly at first, then all at once, until finally I understand . . . I'm in an ambulance.

"Do you know what day it is?" one of the faces asks. The question seems easy, however, as I try to speak, nothing comes out. I feel lost and defeated. I stare at the faces, shaking my head left to right before dropping it back onto my pillow. One of the faces leans over me and says, "You had a seizure." I lie there confused as the blackness takes over again.

That was the day that changed my life.

Let's Rewind

It was a crappy day and I decided to go for a massage. After the session, I hopped off the table and left, not giving myself any time to catch my bearings. I still had things I needed to get done before I could call it a day. As I got into my car, I felt a bit off. I assumed I was just "massage drunk," on a high from my massage.

As I sat at a stoplight, which seemed to take forever to change, I felt extremely hot, so I cranked up my air conditioning. My right leg was tingling, like it was asleep, but I ignored it as traffic started to move again. Then my ears started ringing. Not normal ringing, but something more intense, increasing to the point where I could no longer hear my radio. As I reached for the volume knob to turn it up, the entire right side of my body tingled. I began to hear the voices of my family and friends coming from my passenger seat. I was certain I was hearing things and scanned my car to prove I was alone.

By now I knew something was wrong. My whole body tingled, like an extreme vibration. I decided to pull over; but as I checked my side mirror, none of the objects registered in my brain. As I approached the next intersection, I had one thing on my mind: to get off the road. I began to turn right and the next thing I knew...BAM...I woke up in an ambulance.

After I was released from the hospital, I felt confused and vulnerable. I had severe bruising on both arms which left me barely able to use them for a couple of weeks. Everyone I knew wanted to know what happened to me; but I had no idea how to respond. It was like a fog surrounded the event. All I knew was what I had been told: my car idled through an intersection, went over a curb and gently tapped a fire hydrant. But I remembered none of that.

Best Laid Plans

I decided to ignore the entire incident, move on and treat it like it was a fluke.

Six months later, everything seemed to be going fine. I was doing excellent in college, paying off debts and planning a wedding that was happening in Michigan. And since my fiancé and I were living in Florida, this presented an extra level of difficulty. Stressed, but excited, I boarded a plane heading to Michigan to finalize the wedding plans. Since I don't like flying, I decided to take a nap.

The next thing I remember, I'm waking up in an ambulance again. My mom, who was waiting to pick me up from the airport, was an emotional mess by the time she found me in the back of the ambulance. Apparently, during the descent, I had another seizure.

My mom and I felt it was best to schedule an appointment with our family doctor who put me on anti-seizure medication. For the record, I'm not a fan of taking pills, but I followed the doctor's orders since I didn't want a repeat of the earlier seizure experiences.

All drugs have side effects and this one was no different. It caused me to become easily agitated and aggressive with others. When anyone asked how I was feeling, I was at a loss how to answer and felt the desire to be hostile with my responses. Consciously I knew this was not me so I began looking inward and paying less attention to the world around me creating a reclusive, introspective pattern. And it was during this phase that I learned to truly feel my feelings. I learned to determine genuine feelings and emotions from those that were caused by the medicine.

As I adjusted to this new life routine, I tentatively accepted the fact that I may have some neurological condition that could strike at any time. However, six months passed without incident, and I began to trust the medication was helping me stay seizure-free.

The morning after my thirtieth birthday, I was driving in an unfamiliar part of town when I was pulled over for speeding. I was only going 30 miles an hour, but unfortunately it was a school zone and I was issued a $400 ticket. A wave of negative emotion hit me like a truck. I went from a fun night with friends the night before, to being slapped with this huge ticket, something I couldn't afford.

And even though my father paid the fine, I held onto the energy, frustration and anger of being pulled over and was still seething as I settled down to sleep later that night. The neighbor's barking dog added to my annoyance of another highly emotional day. That was the last thing I remembered until I woke up to my wife crying over me. I asked her what was wrong and she told me I'd had another seizure. She had stayed by my side throughout the entire event, monitoring my pulse and breathing, to make sure I was okay. She was scared and visibly shaken, and I decided right then and there that I was going to do whatever it took to put an end to these seizures.

I'm Done ... No More!

The next day I talked with my mom over the phone. The medication was obviously not working; so we discussed what could have caused the seizures, looking for a common denominator among the three events. Then, all the pieces of the puzzle came together and the answer was revealed — extreme stress levels.

My mother, a former stress management coach, educated me on the effects of stress. She explained that it didn't matter whether something is perceived as good or bad, that stress is stress. Stress from a happy event — like a wedding — or from a negative event — like a speeding ticket — has the same effect on our bodies; and the key to staying healthy, is in how we handle it.

After processing everything that had occurred over the last year of my life, I was determined to take back control. I no longer wanted to be a victim to external experiences affecting me in such an extreme way. I made a declaration to myself, my wife and my mom that I was done having seizures and that I wouldn't have one again.

My mom, being the proactive soul that she is, felt if I was to keep that commitment that I'd need to develop tools to deal with stress as it came up. So she packed up her stress management tools, hopped in the car with my stepdad and drove to see me in Florida.

The funny thing is that I resisted accepting her help at first. I had a pattern where I was so determined to be independent, that I took on too much in life and spread myself too thin. My belief of what a man should be was preventing me from accepting help when I needed it. Eventually, I let go of my ego and welcomed her help.

When my family arrived, we set aside time every day to talk and develop a game plan. We started with simple stuff like taking time to breathe when life is not going my way. Not regular breaths, but breathing deeply from the diaphragm, something I discovered that is not only easy to do, but really helps calm me down. We also talked about the benefits of meditation, which I am still working on but have not perfected yet.

But the tool that stood out the most for me was learning to value myself. I realized that I had subconsciously given my power to things that spiritually had little importance. I had created a lifestyle that consisted of a GO-here-DO-this-DO-That-I-NEED-it-now mentality. My days were filled with mental checklists of tasks that needed to be completed; and the importance of completing those tasks created stress. I erroneously assumed that this was life, and that was what we did as adults.

I asked myself where I was on my to-do list and realized I was not on it at all. Caring for myself was not even in my awareness because I was so caught up in doing things and completing tasks, that I forgot to appreciate what really mattered.

After my family left, my mom and I touched base almost every day, discussing how I was feeling and if anything I felt changed my physiological state. If so, we would brainstorm solutions. I learned to ask questions which helped create a proactive way of thinking for me instead of a reactive one. And the effect on my physical health has been life changing.

Control, Alt, Delete

It has been three years since my last seizure. Three years deprogramming a lifetime of developed reactions. Each year feels more natural when face-to-face with life's curve balls. When an unwanted or unwelcomed element imposes its will in my world, I take a step back in my mind and watch. I watch everything play out around me. I watch my emotions develop and then compare them to what is actually occurring. It's almost like watching a movie or a TV show.

Over the last year I've been put through the ringer of intense emotions, tested in ways I thought would never be a reality. For example, like most marriages, mine has been very challenging lately with many chances to take the exit ramp. This is when my stress-management tools come into play: I learned to slow down, breathe and ask myself questions in order to get in touch with how I'm feeling. Questions like:

Why does this make me feel the way I do?
What effect does this have on my life?
Is feeling this way going to change anything?

I ask whether there is anything I can do to change what is occurring, or if I must simply accept it. Regardless of what the answer may be, I choose not to let the situation engulf me, giving me time to look at my situation from all angles and act from a place of balance.

I've been in awe of the inner peace I've been able to maintain, and the sense of calm with which I've responded to situations that have unfolded before my eyes.

My mind is no longer backed into a corner as situations attempt to toy with my emotions. In fact, I realized the corner I felt I was in — didn't even exist. I had been living in a box.

In a box without walls.

Dedicated to those of you who have experienced the negative effects of stress. I hope my experience awakens the wisdom in your heart so you may live life for what really matters.

Special thanks to my wife and family for sticking by me over the last four years. Each one of you have provided the strength and motivation I needed to get me through a vulnerable time. Especially my mom, you are the smartest and strongest person I know. I can't thank you enough. I love you all so much!

~ D.J. Lawson

Deanna Leigh

DEANNA LEIGH was a seasoned C-Level executive for over 30 years. She is passionate about helping others, sharing her journey, being a voice for women, and inspiring everyone she meets.

She is a published author, international writer, speaker, and sought-after business consultant. She resides in Indianapolis, Indiana where she loves to travel, write, facilitate workshops, and create new projects for teaching others.

info@deanna-leigh.com
www.deanna-leigh.com

🌿 Dare to be Real

I've grown accustomed to hearing the word authentic because we seem to be bombarded with that word in the self-help genre. So I want to make it simple and easy; let's get real, for ourselves and for others.

It seems to me as a member of the feminine society, we are taught at a young age to be pleasing, polite, courteous, and well-mannered at all times because that is expected of women. We are the hostess with the mostest, right? I have to laugh when I say that, because to some degree we are. Whether we like it or not, there are still gender roles, and that isn't necessarily a bad thing unless it's not real for you. Typically, the female is the caregiver of all those around her, giving her the mind set to believe she needs to seek people's approval to validate herself, therefore acts accordingly.

The fault isn't in the premise of this theory or belief, but that we are allowing this to change our perspective of who we are individually as a woman. Our feminine nature usually is to be pleasing but we do it at times opposing ourselves to the point of lowering our self-esteem so others will accept us. Even writing that sentence makes me feel sad because I see it all the time. I've done it too, so I speak from experience; doing this goes against what my soul was telling me. We feel inside when it's wrong, but we ignore it most of the time.

Let me share a story with you. One of my dear friends found this lesson out the hard way. We were best friends in high school, and several years after graduation she met a wonderful man who is a few years her senior. He'd never been married, very religious, devoted in his beliefs, and seeking the same in the woman he wanted to marry. Because of his strong beliefs and the fact that she wanted to marry him, she became what he was seeking in a mate. Keep in mind it truly doesn't matter whether it was intentional or unintentional on her part, but she dismissed what she wanted in a mate to please him.

I believe anyone can be who they want to be in the short-term, however; it's in the long term that it's difficult to maintain this false nature.

I attended their wedding, and periodically kept in touch with her over the years. They have three lovely children, moved out to the country and enjoyed their life, or so I thought by the wonderful Facebook posts and Christmas family letters. She stayed at home to raise their children, and poured her life into making a happy home, only she wasn't happy. She began to emotionally eat to mask her feelings; never telling anyone what her thoughts were until many years later. All these years my friend had to continue playing the role she began many years ago to win over the man she loved. It was slowly eating away at her, pushing her true nature and dreams down inside to maintain the image she started in the beginning of their relationship. After-all, that was the person her husband fell in love with, right? How could she be real now after 20 years of marriage?

Every time she tried to be herself, he'd notice and would often say something to her, point it out, and she'd stop and conform back again. She confessed all this to me one day, some thirty years later after after high school. The mistake she made, how unhappy she was, and how she desperately wanted to simply be herself without judgement because her depression and her desires were suffocating her. She said she was screaming inside her head all the time. She simply wanted to be her real self.

My heart went out to her! To me, I'd compare her life to living inside an invisible jail cell only to wake up every day and realize the cell is real. All I could feel and think was "What a wasted life." I encouraged her to be real, otherwise she'd never survive, never be happy, and eat herself sick. She had to be real for her own sake, her own happiness, and her own well-being. If he truly loved her for her, then being real would be fine. If he didn't love her, and wanted her to conform to being what he wanted, then that definitely wasn't love. She deserved to be loved simply for being her beautiful self; her true soul.

When we are young it seems we don't know better. We haven't lived life long enough to have life experiences; to realize our choices in life can make a huge impact on our lives in the here and now, and in the future.

I recently learned about a nurse who wrote a book about what she learned from her patients before they transitioned.

As a nurse, Bronnie's primary care was with patients who had gone back home to prepare for death. The time she spent with her patients was typically the last three to twelve weeks of their lives. During this precious time, knowing her patients were preparing to pass, she began to question them about any regrets they had or anything they would do differently, common themes began to surface over and over again. I want to share with you the number one regret she heard.

"I wish I'd had the courage to live a life true to
myself, not the life others expected of me!"

Bronnie found this was the most common regret of all her patients. Can you imagine getting to the end of your life, thinking you didn't live a life true to yourself?

When you are in the final stage of life, you can look back with clarity and truth, seeing from the heart all the dreams you wanted for your life, but went unfulfilled. She found that many people had not honored even half of their dreams and had to die knowing that it was due to the choices they had made, or not made.

She shared it's important to try and honor at least some of your dreams along your life's journey. The truth is, health brings a freedom people don't realize, until they no longer have it. When you reach that point, it's too late.

I know dreams are put in our hearts for a reason — call it your purpose, or your souls inner desires/gifts given by a higher power that you are meant to share with the world. Your dreams are uniquely designed for you. Quieting or never fulfilling the dreams inside you is truly a travesty.

Choices, whether big or small, steer our life into many directions. I know from my own personal experiences how important even one decision can be and certainly the decision of my girlfriend whom I shared about earlier in the story.

If you made one great decision early on in life, or even now for that matter — dare to be real every day, and with everyone. That does not mean share your deepest feelings with everyone you meet. Remember trust is earned. But don't be fake, be your true self. Have great courage to live your life according to you, and you alone — not a life for a friend, family member, significant other, preacher/priest or anyone else, but you! Only then, I believe with all my heart, will you live a happy life with many accomplishments with dreams fulfilled far greater than you ever imagined possible. That's what I feel to be true.

It's never too late to begin. Teach your children and your children's children. It's a message to be shared with everyone.

 Beauty is truth, truth beauty,' — that is all you
know on earth, and all you need to know.

~ JOHN KEATS

Dedicated to my loving, sweet granddaughter Adyson Leighann.

To my most trusted inner circle of friends and family who have always believed in me and never left my side when I needed you the most. I will cherish all of you always.

~Deanna Leigh

Dawn Michele Jackson

DAWN JACKSON is a registered nurse, grief specialist, writer and practitioner of multiple healing modalities.

She resides in Portland, Oregon where she enjoys hiking and exploring the Pacific Northwest with her son, friends and family. As well as working with Veterans in her nursing profession she also provides tools to help individuals recover from grief as a Certified Grief Recovery Specialist.

tobelieveinyou@gmail.com
www.dawnmichelejackson.com

Erosion

As I strapped the backpack over my shoulders a smile came to my face remembering how many times over the years I've set foot on this trail. My legs were aching to move as I looked ahead to the forest calling my name. A sense of peace settled into my soul with the knowing that today's hike would bring about some fresh insight for me.

Every Spring and Fall, since my son was just a little boy hiking by my side, I've made the trek up to Angel's Rest in the Columbia River Gorge. Although the name sounds intriguing, there is truly something magical about this place that I've come to love. In the Spring the trail is lined with beautiful wildflowers of pink, purple, white, yellow and blue signifying new beginnings and growth. In the Fall the leaves turn various hues of orange, red and yellow as if to say, "it's time to rest and retreat for a bit." Each season the forest brings gifts of its own to share with each of us who enter this little piece of paradise; I had no clue how many gifts it would bring to me today.

Having hiked this trail many times over the years I've become quite familiar with the winding paths, or so I thought. In my mind, today seemed different for some reason. Without giving it much thought I continued my uphill climb to the top where I often sit upon the large rocks enjoying lunch, a break and sometimes even a nap out in the sun. I found myself letting go of all the thoughts racing through my mind from the past week as I relaxed into the beauty surrounding me. The wind blew softly through my hair as my breath became deeper taking in the fresh mountain air. My heart slowed, my muscles relaxed and I felt my body ease into the earth below me.

After savoring every bite of the lunch I brought with me, while also sharing a bit of it with the chipmunks, I realized the trail was calling my name again. As I headed down I realized that over the years while the trail remained in the same place it also appeared different every time I ventured onto its soft earth. And then it hit me. Erosion! Over the years the trail continued to erode as the rains moved the earth revealing things not previously visible to the eye. Some areas of the trail now had more rocks while others had less. Some trees now had roots that were more exposed. There were a variety of things that appeared different but one thing remained the same; it was and is still the same trail.

While all of these revelations may not seem that important they led me to a realization about what occurs during each of our individual lifetimes. Erosion! We are all born into this little body which then grows into a child, then an adult that still constantly changes for the rest of our lives. While we are still in many ways fundamentally the same person we constantly change until the moment we leave this earth.

Each of our life experiences, whether perceived as positive or negative, end up causing some sort of shift or erosion of our being. Every interaction with another leads to a change inside of us that may not always be visible but as the earth slowly changes so do we as humans. Who we are today is not "exactly" who we will be tomorrow. Little changes happen all the time. Sometimes the change comes from an extreme amount of pain which we endure and other times it comes after extreme periods of joy. What if all these little changes that we experience during life are actually erosions? What if the erosions are meant to reveal our true, brilliant selves?

We come into this world as bright, bubbly babies wanting to experience every sound, taste, smell and sight that surrounds us. Quickly, through conditioning, we learn how to "show up" in the world which often means we begin to hide or cover up some of who we are at our core. Many of us live much of our lives behind a curtain or a mask even forgetting ourselves who we truly are as individual souls. But slowly over time one experience after another begins to "erode" away some of the "dirt" that covers up our divine selves.

Now let us remember that there is always free will in our lives. We have a choice each and every moment as to whether we allow more "dirt" to cover up all that is beautiful about each one of us. We also have a choice to allow "erosion" to occur thus revealing our true, brilliant "perfect" souls. As we choose to release and let go we are gifted with seeing what's been underneath all the layers for years. The "cobwebs" begin to clear and our hearts open wider. Our light and love begin to emanate even brighter into the world around us. Doors open where previously they had been bolted closed for years. We look at the world with a new set of eyes and understand that every action, word, thought and feeling we experience makes a difference in our world. We learn to accept all that is in each and every one of us knowing that all of us walk a path of our own. Sometimes we walk with others for quite a distance while sometimes we pass for only a brief moment along each of our paths.

It is during this period of "erosion" that we begin to understand our true purpose here on earth. And then we make a choice to show up as our highest selves embodying all that we are with a knowing that each day, if we allow, we will come closer to knowing the magnificence of our souls. It is each of us as individuals, our love and our light, that will make a difference in today, our future and the future of our children.

 Be the change you wish to see in the world.

~ MAHATMA GANDHI

Dedicated to my son, Austin who over the years has taught me so much about myself. Thank you for letting me see the world through your eyes and your heart. I am so proud of all that you are and love you beyond words.

Thank you to all of my friends and family who have continually nudged and encouraged me to keep writing. A special thank you to my mom, Judy for supporting every endeavor I've chosen to step into during my life. Not only are you my Mom but you are also my friend. Your love has encouraged me to fly. And to Ed, I'm extremely grateful for your constant unconditional love, acceptance and support. Your love gives me strength and reminds me to live with an open heart.

~Dawn Jackson

Lauren VanNatta

LAUREN VANNATTA is an instructor at UIUC, a photographer and a painter. She was born and raised in Moline, Illinois and currently resides in Effingham, Illinois.

LHVphotography@gmail.com
https://www.facebook.com/TheTurquoiseProject/
www.TheTurquoiseProject.com

The Turquoise Project

I did not anticipate being so upset, and yet there I was in my office, about to have a complete and utter mental breakdown. I thought about the Harry Potter guest bedroom that I finally put together after the start of the new year. I was counting on the 'law of attraction' to be on my side. We had been trying for 18 months when I put the dream nursery together (sans crib). Soon enough, I thought. Soon enough the bed will be replaced with a crib and the guest bedroom will become the nursery. And yet an additional six months have passed, and the guest bedroom is no closer to becoming a nursery. Don't get me wrong, I still love the bedroom and I am glad my husband and I finally put our idea into motion, but sometimes it acts as a painful reminder of what it *could* be, what it *should* be.

The months and months, and now years on end of trying to conceive is tremendously painful, taxing, and frustrating. The grief of infertility isn't so much about not being able to conceive. It is more to do with the dark questions that it raises, the numbness that plagues the heart, and the thoughts that begin to cloud the mind, day in and day out, month after month, year after year.

Each failed attempt seems all the crueler when you feel you have done everything right. My husband and I dated for seven years before we married. We both obtained undergraduate degrees and then master's degrees. We have both worked in our fields of study for years now. We bought a home. We rescued a pup who is happy, healthy, and quite spoiled. All in all, we have followed our culture's protocol, and yet, we still sit childless.

I tried what seems like every trick or old wives' tale in the book. I receive reiki and massages, I use fertility medicine and creams, I switched over to all natural soaps and deodorant, I drink all sorts of teas, my diet has changed, I am exercising, and still, nothing. Additionally, I meditate on it, I pray about it, I have even seen psychics about it, and yet nothing brings all that much clarity or hope.

One of the most difficult things for the longest time was feeling like there was no one to talk to about our struggle with trying to conceive. Or worse yet, people and their "advice". An ongoing list of worthless suggestions one after another. A painful dichotomy of what to do and what not to do. If you go out drinking to loosen up and enjoy a social evening out, someone tells you, "I heard alcohol can cause infertility". Or, when you go out and don't drink, "You know, you should just drink up and enjoy yourself, then it'll happen". When you are stressed out and exhausted from trying, then you'll hear, "Just RELAX!" When you finally relax, a list of things to try, or do, or avoid is given as an implicit way to say, "TRY HARDER".

Then, everyone seems to find a reason to share with you how easy it was for them to conceive. As if that has ever been or will ever be anything but a rude and inconsiderate comment to make. Or, you have the people who say, "Well isn't it fun to keep practicing?" NO! No, it is anything but "fun" after the first six months. As soon as you realize that you are not getting pregnant as easily as the rest of your peers, the joy of sex becomes the chore of sex.

Sometimes it is even difficult for my husband to understand the daily struggle I experience. He often feels that I let the infertility define me, but how can I not? I most certainly wish it didn't, but every commercial, every television show, every movie seems to have within it someone who is pregnant, or announcing a pregnancy, or delivering a baby. Each day it seems as if the world shoves it in my face that I can't conceive.

One time, this is no joke, I watched television for forty minutes and in that forty minutes I changed the channel three times. In that span of forty minutes and three channels, three different women either experienced having a pregnancy scare, announced a pregnancy, or were delivering a baby. In just forty minutes I felt like a failure of a woman three times. Let's not even discuss what a random scroll through social media can be like. It is a never ending display of pregnancy announcements, gender reveals, and month-by-month pregnancy bump slideshows.

It also doesn't help that our culture often equates womanhood with motherhood. So when a woman either cannot reproduce or chooses not to reproduce the question of a female's womanhood is often raised. The question may be raised implicitly or explicitly, but none-the-less if you fall on either side of the spectrum you most likely have experienced a feeling of examination.

As you may expect, when month nineteen came around and the pregnancy test yet again screamed negative, I was a mess. My mind was yelling "WHY?" to the universe. I am a twin, my husband has triplet brothers, and his father is a twin. We were far more concerned about being on a television show than we were about the chance of being infertile. I sat devastated in my office. I stared at the artwork I had hanging on the walls, I stared at the crystals and stones I use to meditate with, I stared at all the things that usually bring me peace and comfort, and I felt neither peace nor comfort. It was as if all of the artwork, trinkets, and furniture were draped in black cloth and everything around me had become visible in only black and white. And for a moment, I had a pity party. Then, I decided to confront the universe head on and ask that stubborn S.O.B. my "Why?" question.

I sat in my chair, crossed my legs, shut my eyes, and attempted to sit peacefully and quietly. I sat asking my question wondering the purpose of my infertility. While meditating it came to me to use a deck of gemstone cards to help guide my meditation. It was then that I grabbed the gemstone deck, shuffled the cards while thinking about my "Why?" question, and then finally I drew a card and flipped it over on the table.

Turquoise.

The card explained the history of turquoise being used as a stone of healing and its representation of expression due to its blue coloring, which represents the throat chakra. It was at that time I knew. The idea had been swirling around in my mind for some time now, but in that moment the universe was confronting me, it was calling me out.

One of my passions is photography. I am fortunate enough to have been able to start a photography business and have a growing clientele. As my photography business continued to grow I thought about beginning a portrait series, but could never quite figure out what the focus should be. As months passed with trying to conceive and my feeling of loneliness ever increasing, I toyed around with the idea of starting a portrait series that focused on women and partners who were struggling with trying to conceive or have experienced miscarriages. The idea floated in and out of consciousness from time to time, but I kept pushing the idea away. I was concerned that people would not be willing to share their stories, that family members would be uncomfortable with me sharing mine, or that overall people would not get behind the series. But that day, when I flipped over the turquoise card, I knew it was time. I knew it was time to begin expressing my story, it was time to start coping through communication. That day, February 21st, 2016, The Turquoise Project began.

To begin, I used my own portrait and story. I felt that if I was going to ask others to divulge the intimate details of their struggle, it would only be fair for me to start with mine. Next, I contacted the few people I knew who either struggled with trying to conceive or experienced miscarriages. As stories and portraits were shared, more and more women and their partners began reaching out to me wanting to share their own story and experience. The growth of the series has been incredible and beautiful to watch. Of course in part, the reason for starting this project was selfish. It was in a moment of utter loneliness that I decided to begin this series; and I knew that by starting this project I would find healing and comfort from the stories being shared. Undoubtedly, I also hoped and anticipated that this portrait series would help others as well, including the participants.

Each week, as more stories and portraits were shared, the more the project continued to grow. I am overjoyed with the response. The portrait series has become the silver lining to my infertility. The responses, the participants, the stories, all give my infertility purpose. It all makes the struggle seem as if there is a reason to it, almost a beauty behind the madness if you will. I travel here and there to capture the portraits for the series and meet incredible people along the way. Each participant will forever hold a place in my heart, each story a lesson of hope.

Ultimately, The Turquoise Project has allowed me to become more patient with myself. By focusing my energy on further growing the portrait series, I feel less consumed with my own infertility. It is as if the project has relieved the pressure of trying to conceive. Each story shared is unique, and each portrait taken is carefully paired with the participant's story. The series has been mentioned, written about, and shared by a variety of outlets. Blogs, businesses, and newspapers have ever so kindly shared the project with their followers and patrons. I am so very grateful to each person who has helped this project grow. And of course, incredibly grateful for the bravery and the courage of each participant of the project. I know what it takes to share this intimate part about one's life. It is not an easy task, but I do feel it is incredibly worthwhile, and it helps many others feel less alone in their struggle. The Turquoise Project page *(https://www.facebook.com/TheTurquoiseProject/)* is a safe place where individuals can share their struggle. It is a community of people who support one another and feel safe sharing their stories and frustrations. It is a place where we give hope to one another, and a place where each person's experience is validated.

If you or someone you know is struggling with infertility or pregnancy loss, please know that you are not alone. There are certainly many resources out there for women and partners who are going through this struggle, The Turquoise Project being just one of them. The portrait series includes stories from people at various stages of trying to conceive. Some of the participants have yet to conceive, or carry a baby full-term. Some of the participants have finally been able to fulfill their dreams of having children. The experiences are vast. The stories are powerful. So, whether you are in month ten of trying to start or expand your family, or *year* ten, you will be able to find a story that relates to you.

~ ~ ~

One month after completing her chapter Lauren and her husband discovered that they are expecting their first child in February 2017, exactly one full year after starting The Turquoise Project.

Dedicated to my wonderful husband Andy and the incredibly brave participants of The Turquoise Project.

Thanks to my wonderful friends and family members who assisted in looking over my chapter and its many revisions. Your love and support means more than you know.

~Lauren VanNatta

Antoinette Coleman-Kelly

ANTOINETTE COLEMAN-KELLY from Southern Ireland is a Holistic Communicator, International Ignite Your Spark and Success Life Coach, "Heal Your Life" Facilitator, Teacher and Business Trainer, and Independent Wedding Celebrant

She is a lifelong Spiritual traveler with a positive, vibrant, grateful, enthusiastic outlook on life.

Antoinette is dedicated to motivating and inspiring people to discover change, achieve their dreams and reach their highest and best potential.

Website: www.lifehealing.ie
E-mail: acolemankelly@gmail.com
Facebook: Antoinette Coleman-Kelly — Ignite your Spark

That Little Red Dress

The day had finally arrived and I was off to the ball. As I added the final touches with the wow red lipstick and yes, you are correct, I am wearing a most spectacular full length red dress, I am bubbling with excitement.

The event was a Black Tie Ball—Casino Royale/James Bond theme evening. Setting the scene at the most beautiful hotel we had a few sports cars, several boats and a helicopter sporadically placed at the hotel entrance! Each guest was individually announced as they arrived and much fun and laughter was enjoyed leading on from the pre-dinner champagne reception to the rather early hours.

The ballroom was decorated with thousands of twinkle lights and candles and a wonderful selection of casino tables and fun money for post dinner entertainment. The music men were all organised. The feeling in the room was utterly magical.

I have personalized my look to bring my unique style, personality and essence to the evening. I always believe a girl should always be classy and always totally fabulous.

A statement necklace
Stunning earrings
Knockout heels
Wow red lipstick and
Of course, the RED DRESS.

This got me thinking about accessorising myself internally in harmony with the external. Ask yourself: Do you spend too much time looking at the external and not enough time checking what's going on within?

 Happiness is always an inside job.

~ UNKNOWN

When we still the mind, magic can happen. Anticipate all the wonderful contributions you can and are making to yourself and the world. Always see the bigger picture and dare to dream and if your dream does not scare you, you might like to dream bigger, wider and brighter.

Dreaming big involves setting goals for everyone whether you are five or one hundred and five, you are never too old to set another goal.

As you are innovative, artistic, sporty, fun and imaginative, therefore you are the author of your story. So chin up, walk tall and straighten your crown, you are the queen of this kingdom and only you, know how to rule it. The gift of life is for you and it is an amazing journey.

My vision for the Ball began a year earlier as I shared my dream with a few selected people and we began putting plans in motion, selecting a charity, choosing a theme and a wow location etc.

 You are capable of amazing things.

~ UNKNOWN

 Don't ever give up your superpower.

~ UNKNOWN

Take time to appreciate and understand the life you are providing for yourself. You are the boss of you. Your belief in yourself, cultivating your listening skills, admiring your patience, understanding your values, all contribute to understanding the self, similar to the knockout heels we use to accessorise.

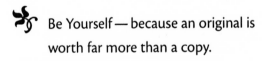 Be Yourself — because an original is
worth far more than a copy.

~ UNKNOWN

Have you noticed that colour is everywhere, in music and sound, the sky and the ocean, the forest, fabrics, gem stones and all foods? Colour is an essential part of our lives and is understood by the unconscious mind. Colour can sway thinking, change actions, can raise your blood pressure, give confidence and heighten energy while some colours can cause feelings of low self-esteem and tiredness.

It was no mistake that I was wearing red for the ball. Red symbolises energy and action and is associated with leadership, power, confidence, keeping your wits about you and keeping your feet firmly planted on the ground.

As I was Master of Ceremonies for the evening, wearing red also enhanced my confidence, energy, inner strength, optimism and determination for a spectacular evening.

Calm and still your mind so that you can hear "You". It is wise to listen to your internal wisdom, your personal GPS — it's a great guidance chart.

Believing in something opens the mind to the beauty of belief and trust. It can help build your intuition and work with gut instinct. Spirituality brings you on a journey to learning new things about yourself, and those thoughts, feelings, passions and sometimes raw emotions help you appreciate yourself for being authentically YOU.

To meditate is similar to wearing your statement necklace, receiving the inspiration and acting on the information.

 Enlightenment is when a wave realizes it is the ocean.

~ UNKNOWN

Along with listening while we meditate for the inspiration it is wonderful to be able to listen to others. As a generous listener we learn about self and life. While accessorising, with joy I realised that stunning earrings represented our listening ability.

 I listen with love to what life is teaching me.

~ LOUISE L HAY

Listening allows others to be acknowledged, maintaining eye contact at all times and actively focusing your attention on what is being said and you will therefore enjoy the conversation more.

Laughter is an instant vacation. Whatever the science behind laughter, it will always help you feel more vibrant and energetic. Make time for laughter. Discover fun, smile always, enjoy company and entertain, and be entertained. Watch the comedy — do you remember the "I Love Lucy" and "Laurel and Hardy" shows? Put some time in your diary for laughter and giggles.

We had so much fun in the planning of this amazing event and indeed copious laughter sessions, and on the night as soon as the laughter commenced, the tension was released and the laughter, fun and frolics continued all night. Awesome music was enjoyed by everyone, me and my knock-out heels and every guest danced and danced until the small hours.

 Positive vibes I send to you always.

~ LOUISE L HAY

We all know attitude is a choice. We create our own world by the way we choose to see it. How about deciding to focus on confidence, opportunity, optimism, solutions, fun and success, and as the positive vibes filter our system, our attitude can instantly change.

 Everything can be taken from a man but one thing: the last of the human freedoms — to choose one's attitude in any given set of circumstances to choose one's own way.

~ VIKTOR FRANKL

If we do not feel grateful for what we already have, what makes us think we would be happy with more? Gratitude is another word for thankfulness and implies a readiness to show appreciation for kindness received.

I have a daily Mindful practice where using my ten fingers, I count ten things I am grateful for, including being thankful for waking up that morning, being able to see, hear, walk and talk, hearing from a friend and all the way to larger and external things.

Right now I am very grateful to you on taking the time to read my chapter.

 Keep Shining Beautiful One, the world needs your Light.

~ UNKNOWN

The Ball was an outstanding success. We raised much needed money for the chosen charity and we had bundles of fun. And thanks to that little red dress, my accessories and my internal GPS, I was assured confidence, splendidness and gratitude for the evening. I felt amazing both internally and externally.

A statement necklace

Stunning earrings
Knockout heels
Wow red lipstick and
Of course the RED DRESS

For you today, in case you have forgotten, your look is perfect. Your smile is lighting up the room. Your mind is spectacular. The wow red lipstick adds your zest for life.

You are more than enough. Share your sparkle as you move. You are doing an amazing job at life.

To-day You can Rise
To-day You Can Shine
To-day You Are Beautiful

Sparkle as YOU Go
To Be Yourself… Always be truthful
To Accept Yourself… Always be Amazed
Value Yourself… Always Joyfully
Forgive Yourself… Completely
Treat Yourself… Always generously
Balance Yourself… Always Harmoniously
Support Yourself… Always be Grateful
Love Yourself… Unconditionally
Empower Yourself… Instantly
Trust Yourself… Always
Express Yourself… Confidently
Believe Yourself… Always be Enthusiastic

Awesome gratitude to my family and friends

For their continuous unconditional love,

Support and encouragement.

Thank You

In Memory of my Most Amazing Mum and Dad.

Thank You

~ Antoinette Coleman-Kelly

Julie Blackwood

JULIE BLACKWOOD is a National Published Author, continues to write books while helping others as a living spiritual guide. Teaching people how to fish vs handouts.

She was raised in Cleveland, Ohio then off to Miami, Florida for several years and now lives in Denver, Colorado with their two dogs Chewy and Lulu for over 10 years. She works in a small business development in the day and helps clients on nights and weekends.

She is driven by her passion to help others seek more than what they can see with the naked eye and to grow as an individual on their spiritual path. Her background includes studies of Political Science (BA) and a Sommelier certification, level one from the International Master Courts. A PhD in the school of life. Living each day with joy and love.

julsvern11@gmail.com

Wings, Shoes, and Fortitude!

"Dad, why do your grandparents sound and dress different than mine?" Dad is smiling.

"Well that's easy Julie, they were born in Europe. You see, you are 3rd and I am 2nd generation American, grandpa and grandma were born here while my grandparents were immigrants from Europe."

"Where in Europe dad?"

"From Germany, France and Italy but mostly Germany."

"Why did they come here?"

"Oh that's a long wonder adventure of a story!"

"Like going to Disney for a week?"

"Well, no, even better!" We both giggle.

"My grandparents lived in Germany and it was a time of unrest and of War. They wanted so much more than what was going on in Europe, torn to leave everyone and everything behind. They heard of a place called, the New world! An opportunity of promise, prosper, life and happiness, they even heard the roads were paved in gold right here in Cleveland, Ohio, America! My grandmother, your great, got letters from a friend who already moved here and said they must come and see this new world. Let me look for the letters and photos from our ascendants. They tell the story so much better!"

"Ok dad, I will help you."

We looked in the attic at the old boxes that smelled of moth balls and a faint smell of rose water from years ago. Things look old, dusty and delicate. Dad has everything in plastic bags to preserve them, to pass down to his descendants (me) and those descendants to come so everyone can remember what he calls "Wings and Shoes and Fortitude" and what it meant way back in 1889 and still lives in all of us today. Dads says the DNA is strong in all of us. Some people call it chutzpah while I call it backbone.

"Ok... here we go Julie."

As I proceed to open the first letter delicately the smell of rose water escapes once more.

Dear Camille,

I can't wait for you, Frank, and Adeline and Gus to come to Cleveland, Ohio, named after some General, Moses Cleveland? America! I too was scared and sad but it's amazing here and well worth it!! We are so glad we didn't go to New York, New York. The roads here are made of brick and some are tinted in gold by some guy named Rockefeller? He found Standard Oil here. It has allowed for manufacturing of automobiles! Mind exploding. With so many inventions being made, making Cleveland this 6th soon-to-be 5th largest city in America!!

You and Frank will stay with me, my husband, Wolfgang and my new baby girl, Isabella. I can't wait for you to meet her. Gus and Adeline are going to stay at my cousin's home, two doors down. Don't worry we are all stuck like glue and do everything together.

Let me know when your shoes hit the ground on Ellis Island via ship. We will drive over in our new automobile to come and get you all. Looking forward to sharing the adventures here in America.

Look up in the Telephone City Directory Book at the pay phone station when you get there, look under Cleveland, Ohio, a local phone operator will pick up and ask for the Cleveland operator, extension 1256 and to connect to my home phone 3787, reverse the charges to me. See you in 6 weeks. Can't wait.

Love you, your friend and soul sister, Halsey, Wolfie and Isabelle. Xoxo

"Wow dad!! I can't believe this letter was to my great grandma by her best friend Halsey.?!! I want to read it all and look at everything in these boxes! Can I? I promise to take good care of it all??!! Plllleasseee! Pretty, please?"

"Yes, you can. After dinner."

"Ok, yes!!!"

Dad instructs us to go downstairs, make dinner, everyone will be home soon from the pool. Maybe tomorrow you can go if you feel better.

"Dad, tell me more!! We can't stop here!! I'll even cut onions!! Wait, what are we making?"

"Okay, I will try to tell you as well as they did can't promise thou."

Dad pulls out homemade pre-prepped BBQ chicken and fires up the grill while I set the table. I quickly make a salad and place it on the table. Then I hurry back to season and butter the fresh corn on the cob from the garden and wrap it up in foil so that I can return to dad and hear more of the story. By this time, I am completely out of breath from excitement and going back and forth!

"Here you go dad, ready!! Tell me more."

They finally arrive to Cleveland, tired from the long travels, eat, shower and go to sleep to explore their first day in America!! They inhale breakfast, their first cup of coffee, jump into Wolfie's automobile. Hearts beating fast and eyes filled with joy. They live in what we call city homes, driving around up and down the streets, looking at the new buildings, stores and churches down to a huge open farm land next to Lake Erie. Frank and Gus are in awe of all of the farm land in front of their eyes. They look towards Wolfie and say "Let's buy this land, build homes, network, create new jobs, new dreams, new lives! We came this far, no stopping now!"

Wolfie says "I know farmers and plenty of tradespeople who came from Europe that don't have work yet." Gus, who doesn't know how to build homes, let alone make bricks said "We will learn then! I know how to plan, create and motivate people! How can this not be inspiring? To help families here to live the same good life as us!"

They all return to their homes where the ladies begin making all kinds of food for dinner and to sell at the farmer's market. Gus, Adeline, Frank, and Camille quickly see what Halsey and Wolfie have here. Gus kneels on one knee on the kitchen floor to propose marriage to Adeline. Frank does the same thing to Camille. They screamed of course at the same time, "yes, yes, yes!!!" But we want our own homes first!! Everyone busts out into giggles.

Dad says, let's pause here, dinner is ready and everyone is home from the pool. We eat the BBQ outside on the picnic table, sharing the day's events at the pool and all I can think of is what is next??! The sun setting now, lightning bugs start appearing and dad brings out a whole watermelon, carves it up and lights some candles. He asks everyone at the table, who wants to hear old family stories? Julie and I have been sharing all day. Everyone's eyes open up wide with wonder, with full bellies and happy hearts. Summer is the favorite time of the year and they all say "yes dad!"

"Julie, where did we leave off?"

"Dad, on one knee in the kitchen."

"Oh yeah, so Gus, Adeline, Frank and Camille get married at the local German church—a dual event. They learn all the rights and wrongs of building their home one brick at a time, employing trades people for trade of their own future homes. Then onto building more homes than they can count. Gus began buying pieces of the farm land, making money and then buying more land. He created over 376 homes on the acres of land of the Lake Erie. Gus and Adeline soon give birth to my dad, your grandpa, Raymond, Uncle Alex and Auntie Eleanor while Frank and Camille have Uncle Walter, Auntie Grace, Dorothy and Marie. It's the mid 1930's now and everyone can't even believe how their lives have turned out so well. All of them feeling so blessed following their wild hearts and are living proof of their wildest dreams and the time of unrest and war returns.

Gus, Frank, and Wolfie often hang out in the garage after dinner, drink beer, and smoke cigarettes, where they normally share laughter and fun stories now share their grief and concern of the hard life they left behind. Turning all that pain and despair into hard work and desire and then into success and much love. The thought of it all being shattered and what kind of world their kids are going to have, wears heavy in their hearts and the ladies felt the same way, drinking wine in the kitchen at the same time. As the days go by the radio had more reports going all day long of the war.

The next morning at the breakfast table Gus, the one with the most chutzpah, says to Grandma Adeline, "We've come this far and we are going to pave the road to the good life for many generations to come, after all, we have our wings, shoes and fortitude that got us here and it's the same that will keep us going!!" Back to planning again. The whole family gets together and Gus's eyes are filled with hope again for what is to come. He says, we are going to have my son, Raymond, take over the family business. He is going to marry Dorothy soon. Meanwhile, Walter moved to West Palm Beach, Florida. He was busy with the invention patent on the first gas stove and continued inventing new things. Eleanor and Grace had followed him because the winters don't serve them and want the year around summer home living as they enter into golden years.

They make flyers, get mega phones, meet the whole community that they built homes for at the city park. As current role models of the community, they remind everyone how far they've come and that we will make the best of it by sharing family stories and leading by example. "Men will go to war as our ascendants before us and will get engaged to their women, giving hope for all. My son, Raymond, The *General* (short for general contractor) and his wife Dorothy will continue building brick homes for the men when they return, they will have a new home and have backyard parties. We all must keep moving forward as we did when we moved to this new land!"

People believed in this hope. So people got engaged, men went to war with bravery in their hearts, and returned with metals, kind of like our wings, shoes and fortitude in our hearts, our secret DNA passed down in each generation. With no surprise, Raymond and Dorothy had me, Raymond, the second, and Uncle David shortly after. We all weathered these times and came out on the other side of this thing called the good life. Your grandpa, helping others with their struggles providing solutions, taking over other small family business that never recovered after The Depression. He bought them before the bank took it back and hired them as employees with full retirement packages. He ended up with seven small business and three homes. I worked for grandpa for a while before he retired and sold everything.

I was more like my uncle Walter. He had the vision for invention. I wanted to branch out into the future called technology so I went to school to learn how to be a programmer and software designer. I transformed reel to reel film into microchip for a large electrical company. I have seven children to pass down more wings and shoes and fortitude! Who knows who is going to be next to change the world as we know it? Perhaps one or all of YOU!

Dedicated to all the people, travels that have made this journey what it is.

I too also have Wings and Shoes and Fortitude.

I'm so blessed to have my ancestors pave the road as they have before me and giving me that direction of strength to be more than just ordinary.

My special thanks to my dad Ray, my step-mom Louella, for always being there. I couldn't be who I am without them.

To some of my dearest friends/sisters Katina, Lil, Jen, Edith, Destia, Cru, Loring, Juls and Joey. You all are the glue in this thing called life. Without all of you, I could not find courage in all the darkness and light. To always knowing the song in my heart and sing it back to me when I've forgotten how it goes.

Thank you for the opportunity to share this slice of my life with you all. Here's to many more years of fun and learning! May you all have Wings, Shoes, and Fortitude.

– Julie Blackwood

Aubrey Rhoden

AUBREY RHODEN is a devoted Mother, Wife, Author, and Photographer. She grew up in Colorado and has spent many years in the South. Most of her inspiration for writing is taken from the essence of life that surrounds her. She believes we all have a story that can be told and every experience we have is preparing us for something greater. Her novel "I am ... " has yet to be published, for more information please contact her directly.

aubrey.rhoden@gmail.com

✿ Moments

As the sun dipped below the horizon, twilight settled in, my favorite part of the day. For a brief moment, my problems faded into oblivion and a sense of appreciation swept over my soul. Dusk faded fast into darkness and, as the moon surfaced, my grandmother shuffled slowly around her large, southern, front porch, lighting her candles.

I closed my eyes and began thinking of my mother and how she always said a series of moments measured life—experiences—so many of which I have taken for granted. There was a moment in my mother's life that changed hers forever. From what I've been told about her first child, he looked like an angel. Our family said he was beautiful, cheerful, and loved by my mom with all her heart. He had bright blue eyes, rosy cheeks, and curly blond hair. "His laugh was contagious," my grandmother would tell me. "That giggle made even the darkest day bright."

There is a river, situated between two cliffs that define the edge of the small Colorado town where I grew up. A narrow path runs parallel to this river and in the summer, people enjoy meandering aimlessly, admiring the breathtaking cliffs surrounding them. There are two entrances into this particular section of the river walk that are about five miles apart from each other. My mother had taken her son into town hundreds of times before, but for reasons unknown, this was the first time that she took him down to see the river. He was eighteen months old.

Weather can be unpredictable in those high mountain towns. About halfway through the riverside stroll, it began to rain; the storm continued to build. The rain came down hard, fast, and steady. The streets of the town above them began to flood as water cascaded down the cliffs. Suddenly the river started to rise... and rise... and rise. My mother was running as fast as she possibly could but the stroller was beginning to float, so she took her son out and held him tight to her chest. I could only imagine the rapid state of panic that washed over her, knowing that if she didn't reach an exit, they would both drown. She told me this story only once, but I'll never forget how she described that moment. How she'd felt utterly alone in the elements and in pure desperation she'd looked to the heavens for help, but the clouds were black and thick, raging with fury above her. She told me how loud she'd screamed, but her voice had been just a whisper, lost in the torrential downpour as the waters began to swallow them. The current was strong, the water cold, the weather fierce and unrelenting. It didn't take long before she was swept off her feet.

Their terrified screams were silenced...

It was dark.

Quiet.

My mother awoke in the hospital room, screaming for her firstborn child. "There was nothing that could have been done," the police told her. "The water rose too fast." When they recovered his lifeless body, he was washed up on the riverbed, ten miles away. They found him lying on his side with his hands gently placed together and under his right cheek. "Like an angel," the police said.

My grandmother always told me how much I scared my mom. "She loves you too much, and the possibility of loss cripples her. She keeps you at a distance for her protection." On each anniversary of that horrific day, my mother walks alone by that river and cries. My brother's tombstone reads:

> Angels will always return to Heaven, no one will ever know
> the strength of my love for you. After all, you're the only one
> who knows what my heart sounds like from the inside.

Five years later, I was born. My mother did not embrace me with weakness. Like a warrior, she taught me to be strong. She agreed with the saying, "A strong mother doesn't tell her cub, 'Stay weak so the wolves can get you,' she says, 'toughen up, this is the reality we are living in.'" God had taught my mother a valuable lesson: children belong to no one. Parents bring them to life, but their job is to teach them to become completely independent. Love them, enjoy them, and when it is time, set them free. My mother is strong, but she was also broken, and her soul faded. Yet profoundly beautiful, if she were a painting, she would have been a washed out watercolor. A masterpiece, but too delicate to bring home, she would be displayed in a museum for everyone to admire, and the people *would* admire. I asked her once, many years ago, if I would ever be lucky enough to know the real her. She said to me, "Sweetheart, you know yourself, and with that knowing, you know me." My mother's soul dwells in a tomb lost in the past, buried alive somewhere alongside my brother's grave. She is withdrawn, yes, but still she remains beautiful. I have grown to accept her emotional absence in my life, but only because I have my grandmother.

I was honored to be a part of such a strong bloodline. The women in my family are powerful, passionate, and above all, strong. As I sat beside my grandmother this night, I couldn't escape the feeling of unworthiness that sunk into my bones. It's funny how certain things in life, such as a scent, sound, or in this case, the tone of light that caressed my grandmother's skin, can spark latent memories buried so deep into one's past. I have one particular memory that's triggered every time I see the light of a full moon.

One night when I was a little girl, I woke from a nightmare. Jumping out of my bed, I dashed to my mother's room. I swung open her door, but she was not there. Scared, I ran to the living room, searching for her. I found her standing by a large window facing the dark, thick forest behind our house. She was wearing a long, blue satin nightgown that cascaded onto the floor behind her. She turned to me, stopping me dead in my tracks. She was stunning. The moonlight was shining through the window, illuminating her. She looked at me, but I felt as if she stared right through me. She stood tall and powerful, like a queen, or a goddess, for a moment, I was intimidated. I longed for her but stood my ground. "Come here," she said in a very quiet, breathless voice. I ran into her arms. She picked me up and pointed out the window. "Look." Standing right in front of us was a white wolf. This wolf, however, did not stare through me. She saw me, stalked me, and looked deep into my soul. I was intruding. I was scared. I clenched onto my mother tighter, and she smiled. "Why are you scared?" she asked. "She is outside, and we are safe in our home, look into her eyes, she is at peace. I call her Pilialoha, meaning, 'to be in a bond of love.' Pilialoha comes to me at night. I speak to her and we understand each other." I was only five at the time, but instinctively I respected their bond, though at the time I remember feeling jealous of their time together and connection.

That night I sat in the chair with my mother, soaking in the moonlight and admiring nature at its finest. The white wolf did not move much; she held her stance, and watched us, as we watched her. I fell asleep in my mother's arms, but in the morning, I woke in my bed, alone. I was no longer scared. My room was filled with the sunshine and my soul with warmth. I looked out the window and saw Pilialoha was gone. I never saw her again or felt compelled to ask questions. My mother and her wolf belonged to one another. There were many nights as a little girl when I'd crawl out of bed and peek into the living room. I would see my mother sitting by the window. I'm sure she knew I was there, watching from the distance, but she never acknowledged me, nor welcomed me over. After the night I fell asleep in her arms, I no longer experienced jealousy. Somehow I understood that each and every connection we make in life is unique, and one doesn't define another, they're just pieces to that particular individual's puzzle.

~~~

I opened my eyes and watched my grandmother surrender into her wicker chair; I could almost see the tension from her body fade. I took a long sip of my vodka-cranberry and found pleasure in the resonating sound the ice cubes made as they swirled around the glass. Together we sat in silence listening to the evening symphonies orchestrated by the many sounds of the South. The smell of jasmine lingered in the thick ocean air, reminding me of my childhood vacations out to see her.

I looked over at my grandmother, and noticed how calm her spirit was. Ever since I could remember, she filled me with enormous hope and belief in the future where broken women can overcome their personal struggles, not only can they be amended and rewoven, but they will be stronger for making choices to change. She says most women forget they have the power to make life-changing decisions for themselves. As women, we often get lost caring for those around us. We are *'fixers'* often too busy meddling in someone else's problems to take the time to focus on our own. Each time I lose my way, my grandmother is there to remind me that women have a responsibility to rescue themselves from the depths of their sorrows and rise each time with the evocation of courage and triumph. It is our obligation to surround others in need with an aura of hope.

I looked down at my grandmother's feet and noticed that I could still see the scars from a night shortly after she and my grandfather were married. She followed my glance and, trying to make light of my focus, said, "Scars are the souvenirs you have for life, reminders that heartaches will soon be in the past. No matter what happens to you, my child, it's imperative that you do not let the sorrow in life swallow you or allow yourself to succumb to the role of a victim. People will take a victim's insecurities and tread upon them like a doormat." She sighed and took another slow drink of her vodka-tonic. I looked back at her scar-covered feet; those souvenirs are a constant reminder of a night when my grandfather nearly beat her to death with the handle of an axe, broke her jaw, and threw her feet into a fire. I remembered a day when I found a letter she'd written to her sister, but never sent. It was folded and tucked into a book of poems. The entire handwritten page from start-to-finish was heartbreaking, but one particular part of the letter was branded into my soul forever:

> *After several moments of pure shock and despair, I assessed the situation.*
> *My feet were burned. I could not stand, would not stand, for the pain was*
> *utterly unbearable. My jaw was broken; I could not talk, and could not*
> *call for help, or I would have called you. My tears are just as weary as I*
> *am, one by one they continue to slowly slide down my swollen face. I was*

lying in front of the fireplace afterward, curled up in a ball as we used to do as children. Oh, how I wish we were children again. I feel grateful to have survived, but I am afraid my soul will forever be tainted. My childlike visions of a fairytale marriage are completely shattered. As I watched the fire that night, watching it die, I hung to the hope of seeing you again, but, with each breath I took, I could feel my soul bleed. I am ashamed to admit I wished I could have died along with the fire that night, for I feel death would have been better than accepting my reality. Accepting that I am married to a violent addict. I am confused, surprised and deeply ashamed. I feel in my heart that cold winter night was the beginning of the end of our marriage.

What would mother say? Please pray for me.

My grandmother described how being married to an addict was maddening, you will find yourself always questioning your intuition, and the overall meaning of life. In one conversation she said she had felt married to his disease and unable to free herself from the prison. A prison she created, where she was the warden, as well as the prisoner. The bars that held her captive were his promises. He pledged to love her, and care for her, and protect her, but every day she sat abandoned, feeling unprotected, unsafe, and constantly waiting for the next battle. Each battle she would fight alone, and each battle she would always lose.

Sometimes she says she spent far too many years failing to accept her reality. Other times she said she thought the years were necessary for her to truly learn the meaning of that lesson because once she figured it out and made the decision to leave, she never went back. She always said it was her choice to become the victim. While he was addicted to drugs and alcohol, she had become addicted to fixing him and addicted to the pursuit of achieving the perfect family. She refers to this now as the vicious cycle of loving an addict. Knowing very well that unless you have experienced this dynamic first hand, the concept is meaningless and will fall on deaf ears.

I broke the comfortable silence my grandmother and I were sharing by asking "How were you able to gain the courage to leave your husband? With two kids, no job, no money, weren't you scared?" She smiled and whispered, then said, "I had a moment of faith. I was hanging laundry on the clothesline outside when I finally surrendered and began praying to God, asking him to send me a sign, something that I could understand, something to let me know I will be strong enough to leave and raise two children on my own. It only took Him minutes to answer my prayer. Out of nowhere in the middle of the day, a beautiful owl landed on the fence right in front of me. His presence caught me off guard, I had never seen an owl up close before, and I froze, dazed with admiration. He looked right at me. In the silence of his glare, I understood what he was telling me: the children and I had to leave. I unequivocally knew that if we did not, my husband was going to kill me. I didn't want to die, so I left."

"Owls ..." my grandmother took my hand in hers, leaned closer to me and whispered, "have been known to come to those who need to let go of some part of their life that is no longer needed. Their presence guides you through shadows, beyond fear and darkness, and helps lead you to the other side that promises light, happiness, and knowledge." She smiled at me, and then kissed my fingertips. As a little girl, my grandmother always told me that I, like my mother and her, have the spirit of an owl, a spirit that has the remarkable ability to fly silently from place to place, leaving only calm water in my wake.

With that, we both relaxed into our oversized wicker chairs, in the silence, on her candlelit porch, soaking in the moonlight and rocking back and forth to the rhythms of the South. I took her soft, delicate hand in mine, and at that moment, told her how much I loved her.

I want to give special thanks to my husband Connor, who is the best man I've ever known, thank you. I will forever be grateful for the moments in life that we share. I hope the stories I write help my children gain perspective on life: know that with love and integrity, you have the ability to set forth positive ripples that will be woven into the tapestry of life. Those strands will be pulled out long after you pass away, and you too will be remembered for the wonderful men you have become. I'd also like to thank Sara Davenport for being my North Star and helping me complete my novel "I am…" To my Mother, Grandmother and Lori for molding me into the woman I am today. To my family and friends, thank you for your love and support. Julie Blackwood for extending an invitation to me to be a part of this amazing collaboration of talented authors.

~ Aubrey Rhoden

Jani McCarty

JANI MCCARTY is a Transformational Teacher and Heal Your Life® Coach. She is passionate about inspiring and teaching others how to claim their freedom by reconnecting with their path, power, and purpose. In addition to her monthly Celebrate blog, she leads Soul Journey groups, facilitates Transformational MasterMinds, and empowers growth and healing through her individual and group Coaching Programs.

A Colorado native, she lives with her husband, Bryan, and their dog, Charlie, in beautiful Evergreen, CO. She is grateful for her life blessings of good health, loving family, and caring friends.

chooseforwardmovement@gmail.com
www.janimccarty.com

Grief's Sacred Passage

 Remember, love never dies and spirit knows no loss.

~ LOUISE HAY

Without Warning

As I struggled to lift myself out of the tub, I thought of my mother. My mother loved a good bath. I immediately flashed back to June 27, 2011 — my mother's last birthday.

She'd driven up to my house and then we went to a charming, little bed-and-breakfast nearby for lunch. I remember sensing a distance, a lack of her usual engagement. Several times I felt the urge to reach over and touch her hand to ask her if she was okay — but I didn't.

Afterward, we headed to the barn to see Peanut Butter, my horse, to feed her a carrot and pet her nose. As Mother moved around Peanut's stall, I detected a frailty about the woman who'd always been my strength and support. It was uncharacteristic, foreign actually, despite her 83 years.

She was missing her usual spunk and I thought about how my father's fall in December, his subsequent shoulder surgery, and his slow recovery over the past six months, had really drained her.

When she headed home in her little red Mercedes, I said a prayer for her safe arrival just 30 minutes away. I was feeling bad that I'd asked her to drive up to my place to celebrate her birthday. It seemed like I'd asked a lot of her, even though she would never have said so.

Several weeks later, my father made the difficult decision to undergo a second surgery on his shoulder. It had not healed properly and needed to be rebuilt. The surgery was risky for someone of his age and condition; and we all prayed that he'd survive it.

Mom insisted we get the family together for photos before Dad's surgery. She'd gotten her hair done for the pictures and was disappointed with how light the rinse had turned out. We all teased her about "going blonde," and agreed that it certainly looked different.

After the photos were taken, my two sisters and I gathered with Mom and Dad on their back patio to discuss their estate. My mother talked about how someday they'd both be gone and how they hoped we girls would remain friends and continue to love each other. I felt uncomfortable hearing her talk about death, especially with my father's impending surgery.

My father survived with steady vitals. We girls waited and played mahjong as we'd done all the other times when Dad was in the hospital. After the doctors emerged to announce their success, we walked to a nearby restaurant for a much needed, late lunch.

We were all very relieved. And tired. But there was something off about my mother, something very strange. It felt like she wasn't really there. She seemed almost transparent. There was no weight to her energy, her hair was very pale and her skin looked fragile, like parchment.

I felt my heart move into my throat. I sensed for just a moment that my mother was fading away. Immediately, I stuffed down my fear and shook off my observations.

We brought my father home a couple of days later. We made him comfortable in his favorite chair and then he dozed to the sound of us girls once again playing mahjong. I experienced such a sense of relief and peace, as the love and laughter of our family prevailed.

Eventually, I told the others to continue the game without me. I had a meeting that I felt obligated to keep even though I had to force myself to leave.

As I reluctantly drove away, I was aware of my intuitive voice pleading with me to relinquish "my responsibility" and return to my family's house — but I ignored it.

Early the next morning on the way home from my workout class, I felt a sudden and desperate urge to talk to my mother. When I called the house, my older sister answered. I asked to speak to Mom, my urgency now in my throat. For some reason, my heart was beating rapidly and I was having difficulty breathing.

The tone of her voice made me panic when she told me Mom couldn't come to the phone. She said Mother had awakened earlier that morning with an ache in her back. She refused to go to the hospital but agreed to have our younger sister take her to the family doctor.

I immediately turned my car around and headed to my folk's house. I had to keep reminding myself to breathe and focus on my driving. When I pulled into their driveway, I was filled with dread and struggled to compose myself before I went in.

My older sister met me at the door and held me as she told me the news. Less than two months after we'd celebrated her birthday, our precious mother was gone. With our younger sister holding her hand, our mother slipped away at the doctor's office, without fight or fanfare. Her heart had simply given out.

My mother's light, her beautiful, radiant light...just switched off.

Questioning My Sanity

 Sometimes others turn from my pain. I hear them offering to help, but I see them slipping away in another direction, afraid to stand by me in such a terrifying place. It is then that I must preciously guard my own process, and find my way, not based on another's estimation, but chosen for my own comfort's sake.

~ MOLLY FUMIA

The shock of my mother leaving so unexpectedly left me feeling lost and unsafe. *Where was my confidant? Who would I turn to when I felt afraid or upset? Who would listen to me now without judgement? How could it be, that she was no longer here to hug me and remind me of how very much I am loved?*

I felt incapable of comprehending this new reality. I didn't understand how the world could keep on ticking, keep on pushing around me, as if no one or nothing had changed. It was as if the grief that consumed me was somehow not obvious, that the implosion of my heart could not be seen, and my loss of all that was familiar was insignificant to everyone, but me.

Just yesterday someone I had not seen for a while greeted me warmly and asked, "So are you better now?"

I admit I was taken back and not quite sure how to respond. It had only been a couple of months since my life had turned inside out without Mother. Had I made progress on my journey with grief? Was I accepting of what I felt now? Was it necessary for me to assess my grief? Was there something here to be measured?

This evening, I shoveled snow. The air was clean, clear, and crisp. I quietly acknowledged the cleared rows of my accomplishment and recognized how quickly new flakes diminished my success.

Tears, thoughts of Mother, and a memory: I pictured her shoveling the front walk of our childhood home. The navy and gold, wool scarf she'd had since she was a kid was swaddled around her head covering her mouth. I recognized the familiar flowing rhythm of her shoveling; and it made me smile.

And then the veil dropped. My heart and head were flooded with sadness; and the aching reminder of her passing, returned.

The snow continues.

Time continues.

I continue, forward... without her.

My New Companion

My grief came (and still comes) in waves—sometimes I wanted to shout at the top of my lungs, or run, or hide. Then, for little glimmers of time, I experienced acceptance and even surrendered to its embrace. Grief, my new companion, created a space for my forgiveness and conquered my regrets.

Prayer, permission to weep, and journaling my thoughts and feelings, seemed to give me some solace. Being in nature helped, too. Whether walking, or being still with Mother Earth and her living creatures; I felt a spiritual connection to my mother.

My father had his own angry grief. My sisters, too, struggled to find their way. We clung to each other in our desperation to preserve some semblance of Mother's presence and loving heart.

My sisters and I took turns caring for our ailing father until his death less than two years later. Though his shoulder healed, he struggled with his ongoing melanoma, and his broken heart. There was such a focus on managing his care and balancing my life that grieving Mother seemed, at times, to be something I'd have to get to later.

I began to feel my connection with her slipping away, much like her life did, although so abruptly at the end. I felt a growing gnawing at the back of my throat. It was like a yearning for a fresh memory to help me remember her. Then one night, my unspoken prayer was answered:

> *Ten months after your death, Mother, you came to me. My precious daughter Hannah and I were at a transformational seminar and we had experienced an emotionally challenging day. We spent the evening in our hotel room talking and attempting to soothe each other.*
>
> *Exhausted, I settled into bed; though my adrenaline was still pumping. My breath came intermittently. I had to continuously remind myself to just keep breathing. Finally I let go and fell into a fitful sleep. My last conscious thought was that of my deep, familiar ache for you, Mother.*

In the very early morning, I awakened. I was lying on my back and could hear Hannah's soft breathing from the next bed. And then I felt you, Mother!

Your soft downy essence was of no measurable weight, yet you had an identifiable warmth and sweet scent. You caressed my face, easing my stress and struggle. My forehead and jaw relaxed; my skin felt soft, youthful.

Your energetic warmth continued down my body until you had cloaked me like a cocoon. I felt safe in your unwavering strength Mom, and deliciously happy and content.

I know I was smiling, Mother. You suspended me tenderly within your presence. I felt your comforting peace and immense love. As I marveled and allowed myself to soak in "all that is you," I drifted into a deep, peaceful sleep.

Thank you, Mother, for coming to me. Thank you for your love and comfort. Thank you for showing me that you are still here...

A New Norm

 I've learned that grief can be a slow ache that never seems to stop rising, yet as we grieve, those we love mysteriously become more and more a part of who we are. In this way, grief is yet another song the heart must sing to open the gate for all there is.

~ MARK NEPO, *The Book of Awakening*

Coming up on the 5th anniversary of my mother's death, I recognize how my relationship with both my grief, and my mother, has changed. Although I still ache for her physical touch, and dream about her warm, contagious smile; I hear her voice and laughter everywhere.

She speaks to me through music and the rustle of the wind. I see her love and beauty in each colorful flower and billowy cloud. She catches my attention by laying feathers in my path, or pennies at my feet.

My mother lives on in me, within my heart and memories. Through grief's sacred passage, I celebrate with my mother—a spiritual bond and an everlasting love.

I love you, Smiley.

Dedicated to my sisters, Lynne and Brooke. I love you!

To all my family, friends, teachers, and clients—I am grateful for your contribution to my life.

~ Jani McCarty

Karen Maxwell, DC

DR. KAREN MAXWELL is the Founder and CEO of Euphoria Transformations and Elite Health. She is an innovative and progressive Chiropractor, Elite Master B.E.S.T. practitioner, Intuitive Healer, Medium and Transformational licensed Heal Your Life® workshop leader and coach. Dr. Karen has over 25 years of experience working with thousands of patients from around the world helping them to recreate health and wellness in their lives. She is known internationally as a master healer, speaker, author and teacher. She specializes in complete wellness where her retreats and wellness programs are focused on changing lives. Dr. Karen has committed her life to motivating and empowering others to live their lives to the fullest potential. Her approaches lead people to discover things that lay hidden within them, helping them to have more balance and love in their lives.

elitewellbeing@gmail.com
www.drkarenmaxwell.com

Peaks and Valleys

 Well, I know it wasn't you who held me down

Heaven knows it wasn't you who set me free

So often times it happens that we live our lives in chains

And we never even know we have the key.

~ THE EAGLES

When I think about life in general terms, I think of it as climbing up to the top of peaks on a mountain and climbing back down into the green lush valleys. As we are ascending the mountain to reach the peak, it seems like we will never get there; we grow tired, weak and our ego tries to tell us we cannot make it. The destination seems so far out of reach and the journey gets tougher the higher we climb. Just when we think we cannot go on, like a miracle, we find ourselves on top of the mountain looking out over the valley below. It is verdant and lush filled with trees, small boulders and wildflowers of every shape and color. We admire the peak itself, how rugged it is with dots of foliage popping through the rocks and eagles flying above.

Our Ascent to the Peak

We look back on our progress and we are amazed that we made it through the treacherous parts of the quest, like when we had a loss of income, a friend became a foe, being in an abusive relationship or maybe it was relocating to a new city and starting over. Then we see the weakest aspects of our journey: the loss of a loved one, the heartache of a relationship breakup or divorce, or a loss of one's power to another, given out of fear or desperation. As we continue to reflect on where we have been, we might see parts of our passage that have complete devastation, such as a natural disaster destroying our home and all our possessions, being homeless or having endured some act of violence.

The one thing we do notice over and over again is that we made it through each and every unpleasant, unhappy, fearful time in our lives—we made it through! We might even notice that we are so grateful for some of the experiences, yet we still hold on to varying degrees of anger, frustration, fear, anxiety, judgement of ourselves and others—and the list can go on and on. Many of us tend to stay on this peak for a while, marveling at our climb and enjoying the magnificent view, but finally we realize that we cannot stay here. We would run out of the things which nourish us and we recognize the need within to release the negative feelings and emotions from our heart, mind and being…and to replace them with love, pure love, unconditional love, but how? The descent into the valley begins so that we may find the answers.

 For this day, acknowledge the restoring power of hope.

Direct that power to bless all that

needs healing in your life,

including your negative attitudes and disappointments.

~ CAROLINE MYSS AND PETER OCCHIOGROSSO

Our Descent to the Valley

As we embark upon our trek down into the valley, we find ourselves still on a bit of shaky ground. Loose rocks and dirt tend to slide beneath our feet, and again we begin to wonder if we can make this trip. The "what ifs" start creeping in: what if I fall, what if I can't make it down because I am so tired from the journey up, what if I become ill with a horrible disease, what if my heart aches again from a loss or breakup of a relationship? Just like the climb up, we somehow find the energy and motivation to keep on keeping on, pushing aside the "what ifs" and negativity because we know once we arrive in the valley, we can rest a while.

As we travel to the valley we start to release the anger, fear, frustration and all the negative feelings we have accumulated from the long route up and we initiate the process of forgiveness and gratefulness. It is still shaky as we make the descent, maybe we don't know how or maybe we are just awakening to the idea of forgiveness and release. This is usually when a new book, a teacher or an unexpected person comes into our lives to show us an easier way to let go and heal. Just when we think we can't continue, we find that we have made it to the valley and we begin to take in the beauty that the valley holds. The swaying of the flowers and trees in the cool breeze, the bees flying about and the soothing sound of a stream flowing up ahead. We know that in looking back and reflecting on our course we will learn and grow from the experiences.

Our Learning and Growing

Once we have rested a while in the valley, we start to reflect on our entire odyssey. We have come to recognize that a lot of what we have been through was not worth staying angry over … that we feel better to just let it go and in doing so we feel lighter, happier, and freer. We know it was in the past and we cannot change it, but we can change how we feel about it now. We just let it go, releasing the angry and hurt feelings out of our being, and start to fill ourselves with love, unconditional love.

 We cannot change the past, but we can change our attitude toward it. Uproot guilt and plant forgiveness. Tear out arrogance and seed humility. Exchange love for hate — thereby, making the present comfortable and the future promising.

~ MAYA ANGELOU

We see the things we struggled with, such as forgiveness for someone who really hurt us on many levels. We wonder why they treated us as they did or why they said those awful things to us.

Then a force arises within and you begin focusing on the happy times together (there is always a few) and remember that we are all doing the best we can; you find that forgiveness starts to flow. Your forgiveness extends outward to many who have crossed your path and to yourself as well. Those angry feelings are replaced with feelings of love, unconditional love, once again.

We also see how we are beginning to feel a sense of thankfulness and gratefulness for all the experiences we have had, even if we don't understand, at this time, why they happened. We congratulate ourselves for a job well done and the growth we have made in just one expedition up the mountain and down.

 Loving others is easy when you love and accept yourself.

~ LOUISE HAY

The Journey Continues

We may rest awhile here in the abundance of the valley, taking in the sights and sounds and feeling so much healthier because of our up-and-down excursion. Resting too long causes us to grow impatient, so we start to walk through the valley, loving and forgiving. Being thankful and grateful and releasing, until we increase our love for ourselves and everyone and everything around us. When we are ready, we come upon our next mountain to climb. Once again we commence the ascent to the top, and so our life becomes about climbing to the next peak and having some new, or revisiting some old, experiences (you know the ones we just haven't let go of yet) and descending back into the valley to forgive, learn the lessons, be grateful, love more and heal.

Why do we continue to do this climb and descent over and over again? Each time we make a trip we learn and grow more and more, and our true being knows that in order to grow and learn to love more, be more and have more, we must continue to make these explorations.

 There's no statute of limitations on forgiveness.

In the presence or absence of explanation,

forgive yourself and forgive others.

~ KEITH D. HARRELL

One of My Many Journeys

I have made several of these journeys myself. A few have been harder than others. What might seem difficult for me might be really easy for someone else. One of the treasures we find on these adventures is that they are ours — all ours and we get to choose how long or how hard the outing will be.

After growing up in a verbally and emotionally abusive household, I just couldn't wait to get the heck out of there and be what I thought of as free ... from the abuse and the abusers. So at age 17 I finished high school early by taking the entire 11th and 12th grades in one year, along with pre-college classes. It was a grueling year; I left at 6:30 am each morning and came home around 6:30 pm. I was determined to leave home, but also to make a better life for myself (a lesson I would have to revisit again). In the midst of all this I met a man (yes, a man, 8 years my senior) whom I believed at the time loved me and I in return, craving the attention, believed I loved him as well. It was a rocky relationship from the start. Abuse started early in our relationship, mostly emotional and verbal, but I was used to that and thought he will change once we get married and it wasn't as bad as living at home.

We married soon after my high school graduation and moved about 2 hours from my home. The abuse did not get better, it got worse, it escalated to physical abuse, and not that this is worse than the other abuses, but it was an experience I had rarely encountered before and it was hard and crushing on my soul. How can someone love another and treat them this way? He always would say he was sorry and it wouldn't happen again. Yes, I believed him.

I gave birth to my first child, a beautiful baby girl. I was 19 years old, and one night while lying in bed tossing and turning unable to sleep (yes, I do remember this night like it was yesterday), my spirit kept calling to me and I finally allowed her to speak to me. What I heard was "I am so sad. I am so tired. There must be another way to live in peace, comfort and happiness." My thoughts were why do I feel this way? I have a lovely home, a wonderful daughter, financial stability and a husband who is good looking and works hard to take care of us. Why aren't I more grateful to be where I am as so many have it so much worse? I excused away the abuse and I excused away his alcoholism and drug abuse and focused on what I was taught were most important in life—things.

As I was pondering how I was feeling, I knew deep within that I couldn't continue to live this way, if not for me, for my daughter's sake. I reached out again to my spirit and asked, "What do I do?" And spirit answered.

The Opening of My Spirit

Almost immediately a friend of my mother's, whom I connected with on many different levels, invited me to a class that was teaching the works of Ernest Holmes and studying *The Science of Mind*. It was made up of ten women in their 40's–50's, and me just 20 years old. What a blessing to be with these spiritual women who treated me with love and respect, comforted me and taught me that life can be filled with love and happiness.

I learned about meditation and affirmations (which were called treatments in Ernest Holmes' teachings) and was introduced to a very special person who became, and continues to be, my most beloved mentor and teacher, Louise Hay. I began to acknowledge and allow my gifts of healing and mediumship to emerge again. I saw the beauty in everything and started to find a way to my own healing and happiness.

Loving Myself and Healing My Life

The book *You Can Heal Your Life* by Louise Hay had just come out and I was given one of the first copies. I was overjoyed and overwhelmed at the same time. As suggested, I read the book from cover to cover once, then went back and began doing the meditations and practices that Louise Hay suggests. It took me over 1 ½ years to get through the book the second time. I have read it and worked with it many times since. I once told Louise Hay that she and her book changed my life. With a smile on her face and love from her heart, she looked me straight in the eyes and said, "You didn't know how powerful you were! You did all the work. It was always there within you."

I was able to finally find the courage and wisdom within to walk away from that violent, abusive household made up of my husband and his family. I had a four-year-old daughter and a one-year-old son, $1,400 to my name, no work, nor a place to live, but I had lots of Faith that I'd be guided right to where I needed to be. It was not easy, but I did it—yes I did it by myself with little help from family and the few friends I still had. I realized that not only had I spent the last 7 years of my life with a person who was totally abusive, but that this had been my way of life and it was time for me to heal, forgive and begin living in joy and happiness. I gave up child support, my home and the businesses I'd created, but I had my kids and thus began a quest that has had many peaks and valleys.

This was just the beginning of more than 30 years of healing and growing and learning, not only for me, but for my children and ultimately for those I would encounter in my new profession—which chose me.

 Love is within us. It cannot be destroyed. It can be ignored. To the extent that we abandon love we will feel it has abandoned us. Denying love is our only problem, and embracing it is the only answer. Through the power of love, we can let go of past history and begin again. Love heals, forgives, and makes whole.

~ ERNEST HOLMES

It's Worth the Trip

I have been blessed to be able to work with thousands of people from all over the world, aiding and helping them to heal from the physical, emotional and spiritual journeys they have chosen to take. Through my transformational coaching and personal one-on-one healing sessions, to my restorative workshops and worldwide retreats, these people are guided to me through others and I have even had some tell me they heard my name in a dream or meditation.

My conclusion in working with so many is that we all have the same purpose. To love unconditionally everyone and everything that crosses our path on every level, without judgement of any kind, without thought of what's in it for me and how can I benefit—just love. The Beatles said it best so many years ago:

 All you need is love. All you need is love,

love, love. Love is all you need.

~ JOHN LENNON AND PAUL MCCARTNEY

To my children, Lainey and Alex, who motivated me to start my healing journey and who accompanied me on many adventures. To my husband John who showed me a whole new path of which I am very grateful. To Kent for willingly joining this crazy group; and to my beautiful granddaughter, Lilla who gives me inspiration every day. I love you all!

To all my wonderful teachers and mentors who have walked the path with me from the beginning, especially Louise Hay, Dr. B. J. Palmer and Dr. M. T. Morter, Jr. Without their gifts this world would be much less than it is. Thanks to the many, many patients and clients who have allowed me to be a part of the lives' journey. Blessings and thanks to all the wonderful souls who agreed to help me learn and grow so very long ago.

~ Karen Maxwell, DC

Julie Hanson

JULIE HANSON is a student of metaphysics and spiritual enlightenment. She graduated from the University of Georgia and has been a flight attendant with the same airline for thirty years, fulfilling a lifelong dream of traveling the world. She loves being home, too, in Alpharetta, Georgia, with her husband and enjoys spending time with family and friends. She adores the outdoors, nature, yoga, meditating, tennis, reading, and creating natural remedies with essential oils. She is an Angel Oracle Card reader and loves dream interpretation.

Jhansondoterra@gmail.com

🦋 Merry Marry Mary

A message from my company telling me to come home for an emergency started a chain of events that almost made my life collapse. The heartache I experienced forced me to cultivate my connection more deeply to the Divine, though. I will share some of my story and how life took me from a mostly happy time to a very dark time and now into a deep, calm fulfillment.

Merry

My merry years were about the times before any big life-changing lessons. I grew up with many great friends, relatives, and memories. I was brought up Catholic, and I'm grateful to my parents and the church for teaching me prayer and ritual. Church sermons didn't inspire me, nor did I believe all the rules, but religion was all I knew. I attended some charismatic church meetings with my parents where people spoke in tongues and healed others with the laying on of hands. The meetings felt odd to me initially, but I eventually loved them, because for the first time ever I felt an etheric connection to Spirit.

Growing up I was always the tallest in my age group, and I often felt shy and awkward. After I stopped wearing glasses and had my braces removed, though, I got noticed for being tall and thin and even did a bit of local modeling. I liked this new-found attention, but agents pointed out all my flaws, which reiterated my deep-down feelings of insecurity. I started to concentrate on my appearance. I learned to look outside of myself for approval and direction rather than within. There's nothing wrong with wanting to look attractive, but if appearance is all you focus on, it can create a void.

My college years were some of my merriest times. I was tall, skinny, and tanned. Life was easy. I joined a sorority and went to plenty of fun-filled parties and football games. I interned for a magazine in San Diego, earned a BA in journalism, and couldn't wait to work in advertising. I longed to travel, so I decided to work in marketing for an airline, but the personnel department said I had to start in an entry-level position. I became a flight attendant for what I thought would be a year for a large airline in my hometown of Atlanta. During training I met Don, the man of my dreams. I already had a boyfriend, let's call him Tim, who didn't support my becoming a flight attendant, so I ended our relationship to date Don. My parents taught me that if I married a Catholic, life would be easier. Not only was Don Catholic, but he was also the most handsome man I'd ever seen and he treasured me like no one else ever had. Oh, the merry years before any problems!

Marry

Life was great! I married Don and we honeymooned in the Virgin Islands. We traveled everywhere for free and saved enough to buy a house our first year. My lovely fairy tale, which I truly believed in, slowly started to unravel. Don told me he didn't like church and stopped going with me. I felt betrayed by the abrupt change. I wanted to share spirituality with my husband and asked him to choose another religion that we could practice together, but he refused. Contrary to what my parents taught me, marrying within my religion did not make my life easier. I stopped being Catholic, since I didn't fully believe every aspect, and yearned for a spiritual practice that made more sense to me.

Another problem was that Don couldn't have a normal conversation with me. He got agitated hearing saliva noises in my mouth. This notion was weird to me, and he heard these sounds in my mouth only. We couldn't talk unless there was background noise and our intimacy diminished. I was embarrassed to share this information with anyone, because it was too hard to explain and still is. Don also had anger issues, and he told me about beating up some guys with a wooden bat at a red light and at a football game. Despite all these things, he still wanted children, but I was afraid of his anger and didn't want kids until he got help, so we opted for a dog. We got a black Lab chow, and I named him Jason, which means healing in Greek, which was what I thought we needed. We called him JJ and loved him, but he also had aggressive tendencies.

Don then got laid off from work and was home every day and became controlling. He didn't take a job for nine months, and we fought about money. I was in disbelief that my life could turn out this way, and I felt like a failure. I continued to put on a good front to others and pretended everything was okay, because I didn't want people to see how my life was falling apart.

Don and I agreed to go to counseling, fortunately covered by insurance. We saw the therapist as a couple, and we each had our own group counseling. One day we got into an argument, and Don shoved me hard and threw a glass across the room. It was the first time he had laid a hand on me, and our therapist suggested that we separate to give each other space. I went to stay with my best friend Catherine, who was in my therapy group. I spent the first night with her and left the next day to work a trip that overnighted in New York. It was Monday August 5, 1991, a day I'll never forget.

I went for a walk in Central Park and was appalled at the behavior of some of people there. Amid their obnoxiousness, I felt freer to follow a crazy desire to sing a song out loud. I sang a hymn called "The Bread of Life" with the chorus repeating "and I will raise him up." I continued walking and singing with no embarrassment or extra glances from others, to my own surprise.

When I got back to the hotel, there was a message from my company for me to come home immediately for an emergency. I called back to see if it was for my grandmother, who was in the hospital as the result of a stroke, but the company representative said it was for my husband. She didn't have any more details. I was an emotional wreck the entire flight home. When we landed, the runway was rain soaked, so I assumed he had a bad car accident. I immediately hoped this might heal our relationship and we could work through everything. I expected to be rushed to the hospital, but instead the supervisor who met me said we were going to the police station. I wondered why and thought maybe Don beat up someone, killed someone, or robbed a bank. I called my parents to meet me at the station for support. Once there I was led into a room with a few policemen and my parents. An officer looked me in the eye and slowly said to me, "With a belt, he hanged himself."

I was in shock and couldn't comprehend that he had killed himself. I cried, burying my head in my mother's lap. He hanged himself in our home and was found by our dear friends and next-door neighbors. Don had never threatened suicide before, and he did not leave a note. I went home that night with my parents sad, distraught, and exhausted. I slept between them that night, holding each one's hand, a night we'll never forget. I was widowed at twenty-seven, and he was just thirty-one. I had guilt and shame after his suicide, not understanding how I could be married to him and not know that he was suicidal. I also worried what others thought, for my life was laid open raw for all to see.

With my entire loving, supportive family and his, we put Don's ashes in the ocean in San Diego. The boat we took was called Morningstar, and my dad pointed out that Morningstar had a special application to Mother Mary. I also believe that when I had the urge to sing the chorus "and I will raise him up" in New York that Don's soul was being raised up as well. I was open and vulnerable and started noticing spiritual synchronicity in my life.

Not only was I was grieving Don's death and the nature of it, but I was also suffering financially, with no life insurance money and only a $250 total payment from Social Security. My savings was depleted after Don's job loss, so I got two roommates and sold items to pay bills.

Several more deaths followed. My dog JJ got loose and bit a neighbor's child, and the parents threatened to sue me. I wasn't in good financial shape, so I sadly chose to give my baby away, but nobody wanted him, with his temperament. My last resort was the animal shelter, where sadly he was put down, another loss and so soon after Don's death, and my entire little family unit was gone.

My grandmother died shortly thereafter, and I found it hard to handle yet another death. I spent my time reading almost every self-help book on the market, writing poems, journaling, and even beating a pillow with a bat to release my anger in therapy sessions. I was also introduced to a man who channeled a pure spirit who was called The Teacher. I had never experienced anything like it before, but felt comfortable with the medium. Amazingly he brought up Don's death without my mentioning it first, and I trusted him. I felt the same spiritual connection with channeling that I had felt at the charismatic meetings. I attended more classes with The Teacher, although not being completely drawn to his energy, but thankfully I was introduced to the channeling process. Through serendipity I was reunited with my old boyfriend Tim, and we slowly started dating again. The transition was easy, since I already knew him.

One morning I saw a neighbor and her young son standing at a police car in front of my house, so I inquired what was happening. Her husband started shooting a gun at us from a window in their house. The police grabbed us and led us into my house, where we were barricaded for several hours, surrounded by a SWAT team. Her husband, who had been on a drinking binge, kept shooting, so the police shot and killed him. I couldn't believe I endured this unreal scene after all I'd been through. By then I had gone through four deaths in six months.

My friend Catherine and I decided to visit a friend in Germany to get away from everything. A few weeks before we were to leave, she was riding her bike when a drunk driver hit and killed her instantly. Now my best friend and constant support was gone also. I feared who else might die and went to another funeral in a daze. A friend of mine made light of the situation joking that she knew she wouldn't be dying anytime soon. She figured I had met my death quota. It was nice to laugh during such a stressful time. Amazingly though a few months later two of my best friends' fathers died of cancer, and I visited both of them on their death beds, for a total of seven deaths.

Hoping to bring some form of happiness into my life, I married Tim a month shy of Don's two-year death anniversary. I went to several self-help meetings and retreats, went through re-birthing ceremonies, and saw the same therapist that I initially visited with Don. Unbelievably she suddenly died from pancreatic cancer. Thankfully no more deaths occurred. Her death ended a chapter of my life that equaled eight deaths in a short time period.

I was miserable in my marriage to Tim and wasn't getting what I needed; neither did I know how to give myself what I needed. I married him too soon after Don's death without taking time to heal, and we divorced. I felt unloved and alone in what I felt was a cruel world. I sat in the sadness of my loss that now included two failed marriages. I wanted to die. I couldn't bear any more agony, so I went to my knees praying. Soon I fell to the floor, rolled into the fetal position, and cried. Through my sobs I cried aloud for any loving Spirit of light to help me.

Mary

Shortly after my plea for help, I was invited to meet another medium, who channeled Mother Mary. That day I met, or actually reunited with, my beloved Mother, and my life changed forever. At first I was scared when I looked deep into her eyes, but soon I felt her unconditional love and knew I was home. My trust in her grew as she guided me to trust in God and myself. It hasn't been easy and has required my willingness, but it has been worth it. My journey with her has involved practicing many deep and active meditations, learning how to embrace all parts of myself with acceptance and love. We are all born with an inner wisdom, and through time I've learned to trust that awareness and you can too. If we listen to our still small voice that resides within all of us, then we can discern what is best for ourselves. Meditation has been the best tool for me to listen and find the answers within, and it comes in many forms. Anyone can begin with just one minute a day by closing their eyes and being still.

I've also learned to be kind to myself, so as to be kind to others, a simple but not always easy behavior. I take responsibility for my actions and I can choose my lessons from a place of joy rather than pain. When we let go and allow life to flow, we are guided to our next best and perfect endeavor.

When I start feeling depleted or overwhelmed, I begin a gratitude journal. Each day I jot down five things I am thankful for and my attitude shifts. I am also very grateful for my past because it has allowed me to be more authentic. I've also created my own personal altar with tokens and beautiful expressions from nature or loved ones that I pray with. I listen and notice signs within the Universe that assist me in developing my own intuitive abilities. If you stay open and look, you will see your own signs. I am becoming aware of my own light and how I can serve others.

Most humans don't want to see themselves or anyone go through any sort of a discomfort, but pain has been a huge teacher for me. My transformation took what it took and everything has been for a higher purpose. Know there is a gift in every loss or difficulty, and if you find yourself troubled, ask for guidance and see what comes your way! Every soul is on their own amazing path, so be mindful when comparing your insides with someone else's outsides. The answers lie within the wisdom of your own heart. And so it is.

To the infinite love bestowed on me from God, Mother Mary, Jesus, Mama Chasca, and Pele. To my parents for always being there with enthusiasm and constant loving support. To my beloved, generous husband, and all my warmly affectionate family, relatives, and friends who accept me as I am.

Devoted love to my encouraging husband, and gratefulness for my loving stepchildren and their sweetness. Abundant thanks to my brothers and sister, their families, and my amazing nephews and precious niece. Heartfelt thanks to Mary and Donna, my best friends and memory keepers who really understand me and always keep me laughing. Gracious thanks to Amy Pazahanick and all who put this book together for bringing this opportunity to share my voice in writing for the first time ever.

~ Julie Hanson

Amy Pazahanick

AMY PAZAHANICK is a professional athlete, author, motivational speaker, serial entrepreneur, and life coach. As the Founder and CEO of Agape Ventures, Amy has built her business and life around the core principle of unconditional love or "agape." She is dedicated to empowering others to create their own authentic "playbooks" for achieving peak potential.

Amy lives in Roswell, Georgia where she operates Agape Tennis Academy. Her articles and books on mental self-mastery, and sports and business performance have been featured in the *Huffington Post* and dozens of other magazines across the nation.

When she's not coaching on the courts or captivating audiences with her "game changing" success strategies, Amy enjoys cuddling up with her two cats to read, play golf, listen to Frank Sinatra music, and travel to exotic corners of the world to experience new cultures and cuisine.

www.amypazahanick.com
amy@agape-ventures.com
www.agape-ventures.com

The Courageous Heart

I am sitting alone on the floor of a completely empty bedroom, in a completely empty apartment. I have just broken with my boyfriend, rented a new apartment, and left my secure and comfortable job to start my own tennis academy. Everything about my life right now is uncertain and empty, literally and figuratively! I dwell on these feelings of emptiness and uncertainty but only for a moment because there is an accompanying feeling of liberation and excitement at the thought of what could be. This is a new beginning. My life is at a crux. I am in the position to write my life anyway I choose, just like the first page of a new book with many chapters ahead. I created this blank canvas and I intend to paint a beautiful picture. "Where do I begin?" "How do I begin?" I ask myself.

I decide the best place to begin is to write down the core values I want my tennis business to embody. One by one, I write down different words that are absolute musts to me. Excellence is the first word that comes to mind. I firmly believe in doing my best and giving my full effort in all that I undertake. Teamwork is the next word I write down. Teamwork is paramount to success. My staff and students must work together. I write a few more words on the paper; attitude, honesty, and responsibility. I scan the paper to see the five words I wrote. As I gaze down at the words, it hits me like a ton of bricks! "Holy S@%$!" The five words put in order, using the first letter of each word spell out heart: **H**onesty, **E**xcellence, **A**ttitude, **R**esponsibility, and **T**eamwork. I can't believe my eyes! Moments earlier, I was uncertain whether I had made the right decision to follow my heart and start this new venture. I take this "coincidence" as a direct sign that I am on the right track. A couple weeks prior to this moment, I decided to call my business, Agape Academy. I chose Agape because the word means unconditional love in Greek. Agape also fit well with my newly established core values. It is my desire that each and every student who participates in Agape Academy feels unconditional love and support. This was a defining moment in the founding of Agape Academy because it gave me a feeling of certainty that I was meant to do this work.

Live with Heart

Allow me to give you a brief of history on my tennis coaching career, which began seven years prior to the moment I describe above. I began working full time at a tennis club where I was brought on as the assistant tennis professional directly after graduating college and playing collegiate tennis. I was ecstatic to have my first full time job. Once I began working, I immediately made goals for myself. My long term vision was to have my own tennis academy by the age of twenty-six. When I received my very first set of business cards, I turned one of them over and on the opposite side of the card I wrote, "I am thrilled to have my own tennis academy at the age of twenty-six." I would make it a point to see the card every time I opened my wallet. Often, I would fixate on the card and read it multiple times to create a feeling within me that it had already happened. I was also lucky enough to have a mentor who taught me the ins and outs of running a tennis business. I was like a sponge, collecting, retaining, and soaking up everything I could learn. Four years have passed since I accepted that first coaching position. Now the time had come to put all I had learned into action. Not to mention, I was narrowing in on age twenty-six.

Fast forward to the beginnings of Agape Academy. I took the first steps. I left my job at the previously mentioned tennis club, and have started to breathe life into my new tennis academy, Agape. I am now clear on the company's core values and on the long term vision I intend to create. Even though I just had an unbelievable moment of synchronicity with H.E.A.R.T, more reality is about to sink in. I have one hurdle after the next.

I still have no permanent facility. I am constantly talking to different contacts including neighborhoods, parks, and private and public tennis clubs to find somewhere I can call home. Nothing is working. I figure anywhere is better than nowhere, so I start teaching at two tennis courts in a nearby neighborhood. The homeowner's association is extremely restrictive over the hours and times that I can use the courts to teach. In addition, these courts have a lock box to enter that only works half of the time. Here I am, a new "CEO", scaling a twenty-foot fence just to teach tennis lessons! Talk about unprofessional! As I am trying to court (no pun intended) new clients, I have to say, "hold on a minute, while I scale this fence so we can start our lesson. Go ahead, throw your water bottle over, I'll catch it." This isn't good!

Not only that, this facility has only a couple of restroom stalls. The number of stalls is not the problem; the problem is they looked like they haven't been cleaned in years! So guess, who has to clean them? That's right, me, the high powered CEO of Agape Academy. The homeowner's association agreed that if I clean the restrooms and help maintain the property, I can use the courts to run some tennis camps and classes. Of course, I agree. Here I am, having left a good job, in a good community, so I could be cleaning toilets!? I am disgusted and unhappy when my dear friend, Ben, who really is a high powered CEO of one of the largest manufacturing companies in the United States, stops me. He is kind enough and smart enough to have the foresight to tell me, "Amy, I want you to remember this exact moment. Notice where you are right now and what you are doing. Take this moment in fully. This will be a really funny part of your story in the future. You'll get to tell people that you had to clean toilets, climb fences, and all kinds of crazy things, just to get your business off the ground. This is part of the journey. You're going to make it. You're going to have a successful tennis academy and a beautiful facility you can call home. You will reflect on this moment in the years to come and you will appreciate the journey of how far you have come."

That moment stopped me dead in my tracks. Ben changed my perspective and he was right. No matter how hard things got, or how much money I saw slowly disappearing from my bank accounts, there was always something in me that kept believing, that kept seeing the vision for what was possible. I was not about to give up the fight for finding a home for my business that easily. I would grind it out. I would do the work. I would put in the time, the sweat, the blood, and the tears because after all this is what having heart exemplifies. The act of showing courage, grit, or resilience in body, mind, and spirit. The journey is what makes the ultimate victory ever so sweet! And once again I was encouraged, at one of my lowest points.

Trust Your Heart

It is now closing in on my twenty-sixth birthday and I am still not in a facility I can call home. I start to gain more momentum with existing and new students for Agape Academy. The logo, branding, and marketing is coming together. The structure of the company and all the legal documents are underway, but we still don't have a home. After scaling the twenty-foot fence and plunging enough toilets, I was able to move into a better situation with four tennis courts, but still nowhere close to my bigger vision for the business. The four courts were located in what I call "the desert". They were miserable to play on. They have no shade, no water, and after a while you start seeing pink elephants walking across the courts. It is a desert! I am certain I saw the only cactus in Georgia start growing next to court one. Fortunately, the courts were in a decent location in the community and I began to grow a large client base. Maybe they liked the challenging circumstances!? You have to pee, do you? That will be a half mile jog to a port-a-potty for you. This facility naturally provided lots of great mental and physical toughness training techniques!

It is now the summer season and I am running camps and classes in the "desert" with success. There are still a lot of additional hurdles, but the biggest of all is that summer would soon be coming to a close and the tennis courts had no lighting. How can I run a successful tennis operation when I can only teach half of the day? The answer is, I can't. I am doing everything I can to stay positive and to be resourceful. I am constantly looking for solutions and trying to figure out how to make my circumstances work! Finally, I decide to make a pact with myself that I will do my absolute best for each person who I coach. I know that if I do that, I will be successful. I know that success tends to have a "snowball" effect. The snowball picks up more and more snow as it starts rolling. The key is to just get the "snowball" rolling. I figure if each one of my happy students tells one other person and then that person tells someone, and so on and so forth, soon enough I'll have a pretty big snowball—and I do! However, I have nowhere to put it! I am faithful and positive during this time. A lot of people in the community start telling me about a nearby club that might have an opening. This is a nice facility with seven tennis courts. I figure I might have to change my business model to go to that club, so I am hesitant at first.

I meet with the manager of this nearby club in mid-July. I have previously been rejected two times by him. I go into this meeting with the manager with nothing to lose. Okay, that was easy because I didn't have anything to lose! It was only a couple days later, July 19th, I got a call from the general manager. Agape Academy has a home! I got the call two days before I turned twenty-seven years old. My dream was to have my own tennis academy by the time I was twenty-six, I made it by two days!

It is now several years later and Agape Academy has had hundreds of tennis teams and has done programming for thousands of students. Agape has been thriving with great success reaching more and more people in the community each year. Today is a very far cry from when I was cleaning toilets just to get a chance to teach a tennis lesson! There have been plenty of new challenges since the beginnings of Agape Academy, but because of the challenges at the outset, I know I can face anything that comes my way. As I reflect on how far Agape Academy has come since its inception, I am also thrilled by how far Agape has yet to go. I'll save all of that for the next chapter!

Wisdom from the Heart

These experiences have taught me many significant things that I know can help you too. There is no better feeling than following your heart and chasing down your dreams. The sense of fulfillment and satisfaction of going after your dreams, whether you fail or succeed is worth every ounce of pain, sacrifice, and struggle. It was Theodore Roosevelt, who said,

"It is not the critic who counts; not the man who points out how the strong man stumbles, or where the doer of deeds could have done them better. The credit belongs to the man who is actually in the arena, whose face is marred by dust and sweat and blood; who strives valiantly; who errs, who comes short again and again, because there is no effort without error and shortcoming; but who does actually strive to do the deeds; who knows great enthusiasms, the great devotions; who spends himself in a worthy cause; who at the best knows in the end the triumph of high achievement, and who at the worst, if he fails, at least fails while daring greatly, so that his place shall never be with those cold and timid souls who neither know victory nor defeat."

To create a beautiful life, life will require of you:

- **Resilience**: Know that making your dream a reality is going to be hard work and that you will fall down many times before finally succeeding. What reasons do you have that when you fall down, they will propel you to get back up again?

- **Faith**: You must believe that the world is setting you up for your ultimate victory if you will just hold the vision and never stop believing in your dreams. How many hurdles are you willing to get past for your dream?

- **Courage**: Not everyone will believe in you. Be your own ultimate cheerleader.

- **Resourcefulness**: You must constantly be looking for ways to win. You've got to get creative. If you keep looking, keep trying, keep adjusting, you will find a way. What new options or strategies can you think of that might get you back in the game?

- **Vision**: You've got to be able to see the big picture of what you are doing. Where is this all leading you? What is the final outcome that you want? Why?

൦ *Focus*: You get to choose what you will focus on. Keep the negative thoughts and people away! *What can you choose to focus on today that makes you feel inspired, grateful, or encouraged?* Look for the good and you will find it. Look for the bad, and you will find that too.

൦ *Heart*: Most importantly, you must have heart! Having heart as we refer to it at Agape Academy, is courage, passion, faith, resourcefulness, vision, and focus combined. Heart is giving full effort even if there is a good chance of failure. Heart is being fearless in the face of challenges and hard times. Ultimately, it takes heart to follow your heart. It takes heart to live with heart. Most of all it takes heart to follow the wisdom that comes from the heart!

Dedicated to every person who has ever chased or decides to chase a dream in their heart.

I am deeply grateful to all of the teachers and coaches who have gone before me and shown me the way. Your words, books, personal stories, and vulnerability have given me the strength and courage to fearlessly chase down my own dreams. To every child who has ever, who is, or will ever be a part of Agape Tennis Academy. Each one of you is my why. To every person who has been in my life, whether short or long term, you have all led me to exactly where I need to be and taught me exactly what I needed to learn.

Thank you, thank you, thank you.

~ Amy Pazahanick

Deb Power

DEB BARTLETT POWER is a Licensed Massage Therapist, Reiki Master, Physical Therapist Assistant, and Massage Therapy Instructor for Lake Land College, Mattoon, IL. She is the owner of Power Therapeutic Massage, Effingham, IL. and is dedicated to providing quality healing touch to her clients.

www.power-therapeutic-massage.com
powermassage@yahoo.com

Spiritual Awareness

Growing up in the hills of southern Missouri has always made me appreciate nature. I was unaware as a child just how much it nourished my soul. Living on a farm provided me with lots of sensory stimulation. Hearing the sound of water roaring in the creek after a heavy rain, the singing of the whippoorwill and bobwhite, crickets chirping, frogs croaking, coyote's howling off in the distance as I lay in bed each night were some of the most enjoyable sounds. The smell of the freshly cut hay and the sweet fragrances from my mother's flowers satiated my sense of smell.

My sense of touch was nurtured as well. I recall towel drying one of Daddy's newborn angus calves on our enclosed front porch in the dead of winter so he wouldn't freeze, and feeding baby bunnies with an eye dropper whose nest had been disturbed from the cutting of hay, and shedding tears when one of them didn't make it. Catching Snip, my brother's very spirited horse, so that he could go riding. You see, Dennis could never catch him, but Snip would allow me to because he knew I would never climb on his back, not after the many times I witnessed him returning to the barn without my brother. He had bucked him off somewhere down the road. Eventually Dennis would come limping back to the house with a few bruises and scratches.

Out of all my wonderful memories one of my fondest is the sight of my father standing out in the middle of the yard next to one of Mom's many hummingbird feeders. He would stand there very quietly with his finger resting near the feeder until finally one little hummingbird would light on his finger and drink the nectar from the feeder. This brought so much joy to my father, and sparked a lifelong love of hummingbirds for me. I shouldn't have been surprised, when on the day of my father's funeral, sitting at the cemetery, one landed on the casket spray and then hovered right in front of my mother and I as if saying, "hey look at me." Instantly I knew it was my father's way of saying he was still with us and would watch over us always. It was such a blessing to receive this special message!

Flash forward five years, I had returned to the family farm and was fishing at the lake my father had built. I asked him for a sign to let me know he was still with me, and simultaneously my spouse caught a big bass. I remember smiling thinking that was confirmation that my father's spirit was indeed with me. I was mistaken. Upon returning to my home in Illinois I found my daughter having trouble keeping the feeders filled. She had been filling the three feeders two times a day. There had to be thirty or more of those sweet spirited hummingbirds swarming about spreading joy with each flap of their tiny wings. I found myself standing at the feeders with my finger extended patiently waiting for them to land, and happily they did, time after time. It was truly the most amazing feeling in the world having those tiny little feet wrapped around my finger, and the closest I had felt to my a since he had passed.

This was my first encounter with a Spirit Guide, but fortunately not my last. I began to be more observant of the Spirit Guides that crossed my path. I began to acknowledge them and learn what special message they had for me. The hummingbird teaches me to open my heart and to allow more joy to flow into my heart and into my life, increasing the emotional sweetness.

My next encounter with Spirit Animal was the Red Tail Hawk, who taught me to have greater perspective and to observe situations, then react quickly. Watching the Hawk perched on a high line, fence post or top of a tree would remind me to take some time to reflect on the current issue I was facing. More than that it was a feeling that would come over me each time I would see one. I knew I wasn't alone. I had Spirit Guides with me. I began to feel empowered and the stressors of my life would fade away.

I have had several visitors through the years and I always take the time to stop and reflect and learn what the special message from them is. Sometimes I am surprised at how appropriate they are for the current situation I am faced with. We all need quiet times of reflection and getting out in nature and becoming aware of our surroundings is a good way to start. I encourage you to open your eyes, look for those animal guides that are bringing insight to any problems or struggles you may be facing. It is empowering when you are feeling lost or helpless. Call on them or just close your eyes and imagine them, visualize every detail and allow their energy to permeate through every cell of your body, giving you exactly what you need.

One late spring morning while working at my office, I was feeling stuck both physically and energetically, just trying to make it through my busy work day, when I am visited by another friendly Spirit Guide, a Praying Mantis. He was looking down on me from the ceiling trying to get my attention and impart his wisdom on me. When a Praying Mantis shows up you should make prayer, meditation or contemplation part of your day, incorporating some Tai Chi or Yoga into your daily practice! I did some Yoga stretches and took a quick stroll outside and found my mood had lifted and the rest of my work day went by smoothly. It completely changed my attitude!

My blue jay encounter was in the dead of winter. I heard a loud thump at my front door, when I opened it to see what it was, there was a stunned blue jay laying on my porch. As I picked it up to assess it, he let out a shrill alarm sound as if saying to me "put me down." I started giving him Reiki and he immediately calmed down realizing that I wasn't going to hurt him. After channeling Reiki for a few minutes I gently placed him in the shrubs and went to shower for work. I checked again before leaving the house and he had flown off having recovered from the trauma of flying head first into my door. I knew he too had a message for me! As a Reiki Master I have an interest in the metaphysical realm and have dabbled in various subjects. His message: "Stop dabbling in the spiritual/metaphysical world and choose a path to explore and go as far as you can with it." How wise our Animal Spirit Guides are! So if an animal repeatedly shows itself to you, be aware, listen to them, and *learn* from them for they are very wise!

Visits from Spirit Animals can also be a way for us to connect with our loved ones who have transitioned. My dear friend Lisa had shared with me her special connection to her grandmother, and every time she sees a ladybug she feels that her deceased grandmother's Spirit is with her. While we were in Sedona one year we decided to hike one of the many wonderful trails. We stepped out of the jeep, donned our hiking shoes, Lisa looks down on the paper she was holding in her hand, and there bigger than life was ... you guessed it - a ladybug! I will never forget the squeal she let out. We hugged one another and cried. Words could not express the emotion we both felt, and no words were needed! We both realized the significance of this ladybug. After acknowledging this wonderful visit, we trekked on, only to have a hummingbird circle my head! This heightened all of my senses and allowed me to feel the connection with both of my deceased parents. It was truly one of the most magical moments of our lives having our Ancestral Spirit Guides visit us at the same time. You know what? That little hummingbird followed us for most of our hike that day! I would see him perched atop a tree or flying past, spreading joy with each flap of those tiny wings.

Recently I stepped out my back door and found a toad at my feet. I bent down and stroked the length of his back several times, and he just sat there! I took a deep breath and asked Mr. Toad "What is your message for me?" I keep my Animal Spirit Guide book by Steven D. Farmer Ph.D at my office, so I was anxious to get to work that day to see what the toad's message was. Upon pulling into my office I find my ex-husband's vehicle and construction trailer in the parking lot. Unbeknownst to me, the owners of the building had hired him to remodel the adjacent offices. I quickly opened the book to learn his poignant message…."You'll have the opportunity to review and clear some emotional issues from the past." Needless to say the irony of the toad's message was not lost on me. Emotional baggage can stick with us for many years and we need to know and believe that we have the control to change old patterns or ways of thinking. Visits from my Animal Spirit Guides provide me with a sense of calming peace and joy, which allows me to move forward in life.

So when I see a field full of turkeys, it's a reminder to honor our Mother Earth, and focus on family, and when raccoons show up to drink the nectar from my hummingbird feeders and clumsily knock them down, I try not to be annoyed but rather realize that it is my ancestors trying to get their messages through to me. Instead of coiling in fear when I see a snake, I know a long standing issue will soon be resolved. Our Animal Spirit Guides are out there for all of us. I encourage you to call on them when you need some assistance, You are not alone.

Dedicated to my mother and father.

Special thanks to Tom Tessereau for being such a wonderful mentor and helping me open my spiritual eye.

~ Deb Power

Jennifer Wadsworth

JENNIFER WADSWORTH is an award-winning medical journalist, author, and alchemist. Following a successful career in broadcasting and healthcare marketing, she switched gears to become a certified aromatherapist, yoga instructor and Reiki Master. Jennifer is passionate about helping others achieve mind-body balance and tap into their intuition as a daily compass for realizing a divinely orchestrated and exquisite life.

An entrepreneur and inventor, the native Atlantan owns Wadsworth Communications and Naturoil Skin Solutions, a boutique skincare company specializing in hand-made organic health and beauty products. A long-time student of eastern and western philosophy, Jennifer dedicates her life to helping heal the human spirit.

info@naturoilskin.com
www.naturoilskin.com

The Art of Being in Midair

It's a long climb to the top of the pole, 32 feet to be exact, and it's the height of the summer. I am in the middle of the Ocoee, Tennessee woods feeling the heat. That's because I'm next in line to climb the Pamper Pole, one of eight challenges in a high ropes obstacle course, our boss is convinced will inspire confidence and leadership skills in our team. But so far, all I am experiencing on this weekend retreat with my YMCA co-workers is a whole lot of whining, blisters and bug bites. I feel like a kid at my first summer camp, except it's worse. *There's no one to write home to or beg to come and get me!*

Now if you are wondering why they call this challenge the Pamper Pole, it is because it turns grown people into big cry babies who wish they were wearing diapers once they get up there. Church-run ropes courses call it "the Leap of Faith." *But here's what it really is.*

The Pamper Pole is literally an old wooden utility pole with a very small and unstable 4"x4" square piece of pine wood (more like a wobble board) loosely nailed to the top of it *to terrify you.* Once you manage to shimmy up it and arrive on the postage stamp of a platform, your challenge is to find your balance long enough to be able to leap into the air and attempt, *the emphasis here is on attempt,* to grab a trapeze that is intentionally set too far away for you to reach — about 11 feet. Now of course, you are safely hooked into a harness with a belay rope and are wearing a helmet. But still — *it's scary.* Our beefcake of a fitness instructor, who can do 50 pull-ups without blinking an eye, has just fallen short of the trapeze. And now it's my turn.

The Leap of Faith

As I make my ascent, I am thinking *well, if he couldn't do it, there's no way I can. He's totally more fit than I am, he's taller than I am.* He is this, he is that. But **SOMEHOW,** I manage to pull myself onto the platform, and with trembling legs I stand, and **I AM PARALYIZED.** *I'm not going anywhere.*

Below me, my coworkers are shouting, "Jump Jen, jump. You can do it." I've made it to this safe, unsafe spot and I am not motivated to leap into the air or cross that chasm between me and the metal bar that is trying to show me what mettle I am made of. *And then the unspeakable happens.*

I hear him before I see him. The bumble bee that is buzzing by my ear now and boldly brushing against the damp, loose tendrils of my hair that have escaped my helmet. Suddenly all bets are off. ***This is war***. *How dare he break my concentration.*

The bee circles my head, dipping and dive bombing me. Swatting and shooing him away, I am tipping dangerously to the left and now to the right. *My choice is clear.* I close my eyes and spring from the unsafe, safe place. My sweaty palms and arms outstretched towards the shiny trapeze. And when I open them, I see with great surprise, I am gripping the bar firmly beneath my fingers. My hands haven't slipped nor have I fallen. I am smiling. Laughing actually. *I have made it safely with seemingly no effort other than to launch and let go!*

Free Falling

Twenty years later, I don't really know how I did what I did. What I do know is that at some point, the discomfort I felt with staying where I was on that trick board began to outweigh the risk I felt would accompany my jumping into the open air and free falling.

This experience has never left me nor the kindred flight of fancy and quieting of fear that I fantasize I must share with the trapeze artist. The aerialist who for a moment finds herself suspended in midair having let go of the trapeze she has so skillfully swung from but not yet grasping the new one. Not knowing if she will succeed or shamefully fall from grace. *Still, she lets go.*

I believe we all share something in common with the high air acrobat. We share the leaps and the pauses in life and the moments where we hold our breath as we transition from one place to another. Rarely are we comfortable being in midair suspended between where we have come from and where we want to be. *We dislike the pause.* Because it is in the pause that our biggest fears begin to bubble up, and we question our movements and choices. Why did I get divorced, why did I change jobs? Why have I done this to myself? *Who is going to catch me if I fall?*

But it is in these prophetic life pauses and places of uncertainty that you will find your greatest power. I call this place where inertia meets momentum the "*grace space*" and it is our soul's ability to overcome the accompanying fear that allows us to master the *art of being in midair.*

You know the place. It's the hollow where you find yourself when your career, your child or your relationship isn't progressing like you had hoped. Perhaps you are grieving the loss of a loved one, have been blindsided by a betrayal, or your finances are falling apart.

During these extreme challenges, it feels as if time begins to slow and even stand still for the requisite recalibration. No matter how you have arrived here, I can promise you the grace space is not a place where you will stagnant but *one where you will soar*. **I know because I have been there.**

Welcome to the Grace Space

The first time came when my marriage to my husband of ten years began disintegrating. He had a drinking problem. He had an anger problem. And he had an honesty problem. And so we went to a marriage therapist and *got absolutely nowhere.* Our two boys were little and gratefully oblivious to most of what was happening and the mounting tension in our home. I grew tired of his lying and the losing of jobs. On the day I tell my husband I want a divorce, he corners me in the dining room and starts cursing at me. Then he goes downstairs to where he keeps his guns and gets something and leaves the house. I remember my therapist telling me, "Some men are too dangerous to divorce. You are better off staying." And my husband was almost too dangerous to leave. *Almost.* But I did it anyway. I left while he was out of town and took two pieces of furniture and my two kids. I didn't have a job and I didn't know how I would pay my bills, but I knew I had to get out of that marriage or I would slowly die anyway.

The place I found for us to live was tiny, and my oldest son wanted to know, "What is this mouse house mom?" Even though it was smaller than what we had lived in, it was mine, and it felt safe. During the first few months of my departure, my husband alternated between begging me to come home and threatening to bash my head in. He held the children hostage and returned them days later than he was supposed to after his custodial time. *It was a nightmare.*

Grace Comes Calling

And in the middle of this hell, I remember my phone ringing. I was in the grocery store when Dr. Clark called. He had tried to hire me as his marketing director the year before but we couldn't agree on compensation. He didn't even say hello, "What's it going to take for you to come work for me Jen?" he asked. And without hesitation, I gave him a figure. He said he couldn't go that high the first year but he promised he would in a year, and he kept his word.

Fast forward another eight months and I am interviewing some website designers. When the sales rep for the third company tells me his last name, I recognize the surname. It is the last name of the boy named Sam who was my best friend from the time I was 13 until about 22 years old. I ask him if he is related. "Well yes, he's my older brother," the sales rep says.

Wonderful memories begin to flood my mind and I tell him to say "hello" to Sam for me. I have not seen or spoken to him in almost 20 years. But then something miraculous happens. Not less than 24 hours later, Sam calls. His voice is such a welcome sound. We meet for lunch and then we begin to talk for hours at night after I have put the children to bed. He is kind and gentle and listens with such care and concern about my fears for my family and my future. We begin dating and two years later, I marry my best friend and our children become best friends.

I know I would not be here today and have found the love that was meant for me without having landed in the grace space. Sometimes we go willingly and others times we have to be shoved. Either way, it is in the grace space where God gets to fill in the blank. And, he will divine what is next for you, *if you will allow it*. Because he knows what is in your greatest good. He knows your soul even better than you do. God knows why you are here and what you need to be complete and he is bringing you all that you have asked for and more. You may not know what this midair pause means for you, *but you can be certain God is using it for something.*

Loosen your grip.

Allow someone else to light the path. Like the airport wing walkers, who stand on the tarmac with their orange wands motioning to the pilot where he should aim the plane, you have to let go and allow yourself to be guided. *You have to let God be your wing walker.*

The Hungry Caterpillar

It is one of the toughest lessons you will ever learn, but the next time you find yourself in midair (*and you will*), the wisest choice you can make is not to resist or run, but embrace it. *Celebrate it.* Because being here means opportunity and *metamorphosis* are coming your way. Like the caterpillar who builds a cocoon around her body and begins to reorganize her cells so she can burst forth with wings and fly, you too are reorganizing your life. You too will grow wings and fly with your wing walker by your side. And like the caterpillar, you may appear to be or even feel lifeless during this transformation. But trust me, *you are not.*

Now, when I find myself suspended in midair, I recognize the beautiful symbolism of the bee. When my mind becomes weighted down with worry and my thoughts circle in self-criticism, I choose to ignore these "buzzing" thoughts. I know that when I find myself in the grace space, I don't have to be afraid because I've created a wide open invitation for God to enter my life. I don't have to know how I will be able to grab the trapeze bar or find a higher paying job or heal my illness, and neither do you. *We only have to use our faith until we can reach a place of certainty again.*

Sounds simple right? But let's be real. It's not. How do we manage all the worry and anxiety while we wait? The key to soaring in midair is to live with Spirit in the space where you are feeling vulnerable. Don't give doubt any room to creep in.

Whatever you do, don't isolate. Practice giving back where you are lacking. Help someone else who is in the same situation. Even if you can't fix your problem right now, it's rewarding to help someone else progress in their struggle.

Until then, here are some strategies that will help you find peace in the pause and master the art of being in midair.

8 Tips for Mastering the Art of Being in Midair

Repeat This Affirmation: All is well. Everything is working out for my highest good and from my situation only good will come.

1. Forgive yourself for whatever circumstance has brought you to the grace space. If you're here, you're getting ready to have a breakthrough. Congratulations!
2. Make a God box—put the problem/s in the box. Give it over to God and check the box in three months to see how it is being resolved for you.
3. Go to your comfort place—church, synagogue, nature walks, water, music, take a drive, travel or volunteer until you are past the pause.
4. Meditate to remove all your mental noise. Be still and allow God's and your angel's information to flow into your life with clarity and confidence.
5. Journal your feelings. You will love looking back on these entries that chart your soul's growth.
6. Take care of your body. Eat well, exercise and rest. Surround yourself with friends who make you laugh.
7. Write a mission statement for this next chapter of your life. Don't hold back. Claim it, declare it, be it even before others can see it.
8. Write a letter of gratitude thanking God for guiding you in the grace space.

Launch and Let Go

As you create your own magnificent experiences, expect that you may often find yourself in midair. Instead of defaulting into fear, **rest in the certainty that when you move, the universe moves.**

Embrace this important time in your growth and destiny. It is in the grace space that you will find your greatest power and gather your focus and creativity to claim the life you know was meant for you, *the one you really want.*

Just launch and let go. Take a wild leap into the unknown. And let your heart be free as you *soar on the wisdom of your wing walker.*

Dedicated to my golden-hearted guardian and soul mate, Samuel Srochi.

Special acknowledgment goes to my children, Addison and Gabriel, who grew my heart overnight the day they were born and have been my greatest teachers ever since. I would also like to extend a special thank you to my neighbor, friend and soul sister, Amy Pazahanick. What a joy it is to have worked on this compilation book together and to always challenge each other to "go big or go home." Lastly, I thank A Course in Miracles for reminding me that I have but one purpose here. I have only to be the presence of love.

~ Jennifer Wadsworth

Damien Munro

DAMIEN MUNRO is a Metaphysical Teacher, Coach and Motivational Speaker from Melbourne, Australia. He's travelled throughout Europe, Asia and Australia teaching the principles of Self Love and Acceptance, assisting hundred of people — just like you, to discover their life purpose and live the life of their dreams.

Damien believes you deserve to live a life filled with love, joy and happiness.

Having met, trained and worked with some of the most popular and respected metaphysical teachers of our time, including; Louise L. Hay (You Can Heal Your Life), Doreen Virtue (Messages from Your Angles) and Lillian Too (Feng Shui Academy Malaysia).

When you meet with Damien expect to have a transformational experience, bring clarity, ease and a state of grace to your world.

Want to eliminate belly fat, increase energy levels & feel healthier than 10 years ago? Get Damien's Healthy Living Guide free at www.DamienMunro.com/WisdomGift.

Stay beautiful!

Restoring Perfect Health

It was Charlotte Gerson, daughter of famous juicing and health Pioneer Dr. Max Gerson and founder of Gerson therapy, speaking on the mind-blowing documentary *Food Matters*, who said…

> "You cannot heal selectively. You cannot treat one disease and leave two untreated".

Your whole body wants to be healed, whole and healthy. It will not treat one health problem and leave the rest untreated!

Let me introduce myself… I'm Damien Munro and my friends often refer to me as the "Make sh*t happen guy." Look, I acknowledge it's a crazy *aka*, it really isn't my doing though. It came about a few years ago when catching up with friends for dinner and playing a game of how you'd describe each other to a complete stranger. It's a longer story than that so I won't bore you with the details here.

But … I've been in and out of the health and wellness industry for over 12 years. During this time I've had the privilege of meeting and working with some of the most amazing metaphysical and health leaders in the world. Seeing the passion they had for improving the health and wellbeing of the planet sparked my own healing journey and the need for me to share it with the world.

Over the past decade I've worked in Advanced Para-Medical Skin Correction (tongue twister I know), Nutrition, Kinesiology, Equine (horse) Massage, Hypnotherapy and as a Heal Your Life (Louise L. Hay) Workshop Leader and Coach. Because of the vast and varied (some may even say bizarre) roles I've had, each one a stepping stone to my own healing journey. And, although this is only a short chapter, I've had the privilege of seeing thousands of people's lives change from the information I'm giving you here. Even if you take just one thing to improve the quality of your life, then my job here is done.

On a personal level, I spent many years living with acne, a chronic skin condition. My whole face was covered with cysts, and at one time I couldn't even stand to look in the mirror. It was painful, swollen, and filled with a burning sensation at all times. I hated what I saw. I also suffered with asthma. It was so bad in my early years that I was taking the blue inhaler (the reliever) 10 to 15 times per day. I wasn't allowed to run for fear of an asthma attack and limited in the activities I could do. I also had extreme eczema that covered my legs and I'd scratch all night in bed until my legs bled. I remember waking up one morning and seeing what looked like a murder scene on my sheets.

On top of this, the straw that broke the camel's back (literally) ... hay fever! Like so many diseases, there's a variety of symptoms that vary widely. From slightly itchy/watery eyes, raspy throat, headaches and mild sinus problems.

So that was me! All the doctors could tell me at the time was "Don't worry, it's expected that if you have asthma, you'll also have eczema and hay fever. Take these and you'll get relief".

I didn't want relief! I wanted answers. All of this was happening to me from the age of 15 and I knew that there had to be another way. I spent many, many years researching my own condition to find natural treatments. I knew there had to be something more than just another prescription. Conventional medicine was failing me.

I am not Anti-Doctor or Anti-Pharma.

Although what I'm sharing with you has helped restore my health and I've continued to share it with my private clients, I'm not against the medical profession. Far from it! In fact, if a serious injury where to happen, let's take for instance a broken bone ... the last thing I'd do is call my herbalist. My herbalist isn't equipped with resetting and realigning bones. So, I'd definitely be going to the emergency room for a doctor to repair that!

Please consult your doctor before you undertake any dramatic changes in your eating or lifestyle and please DO NOT come off any medication without consulting your doctor first.

Mind/Body Connection

Our body is a reflection of our minds. Have you noticed when you're stressed you hold tension in your shoulders, neck and jaw? If we hold on to that tension for a long period of time it slows the movement of blood, lymph and neural messages through that area and eventually turns into a pain and resulting injury. The ancient Chinese refer to this system as the Meridians and the Yogic Masters spoke of the Nadi's. The aches, pains and illnesses in our bodies often reflect mental/emotional patterns that are happening inside of us. If we can understand these patterns, it will help us transform our physical bodies.

Bringing mindfulness to the aches and pains in our body will often bring us relief and quite rapidly. When we learn to release the emotion that's creating the disease, the new personality no longer needs it and will simply let it go!

A Course In Miracles tells us that we have the right and power to be healed if that's what we choose. Choice is the cornerstone of all experience. If you can release from your mind the idea that certain things are necessary before you can be well, then the healing you thought was impossible is available to you now! Think about that ... If you let go of the idea that something must happen in order for healing to occur, then it will.

Ask these questions:

- What is it I'm getting from being unwell or by having this condition right now?
- What would have to happen in order for me to let it go?

Is it really possible?

Just in case you feel healing isn't possible by just using your mind, you're not alone. And that's okay! All healing is faith healing. We have to put our trust and faith into something. If you're in need of healing, confidently step toward what will give it to you. I've used and still continue to use proven methods to create physical wellbeing and healing. Each of which have worked for me. For you, they may be a doctor, coach, priest, shaman, massage therapist, Reiki practitioner or whatever helps you align to your wellness. For me, I've used the below methods along with the Mind/Body connection to create wellness in my body, heal from eczema, alleviate acne, and completely remove all symptoms of hay fever.

A Tested Prescription for Health

My current practices to create perfect health in my body include the following; regular exercise, vegetarian/mostly vegan diet, raw juicing, Gerson coffee enemas, mindfulness/spiritual thought practices, meditation and regular yoga. Each of these activities feeds into one another and creates a positive feedback loop. Over time, I've tried many, many different things and have chosen what works well for me. If you're just starting out on the journey, simply be willing to learn as much as you possibly can. When you come across something that's strange and a bit out there, look into it a little more. Quite often it's the weird and wonderful that restores the most faith. So here's what I do and invite you to give a try.

Vegetarian, Say What?

Everything in life came to a screaming halt! I was exhausted, suffering from a foggy head and couldn't think clearly. I'd been practicing yoga, mindfulness and meditation for years. "Why wasn't I beaming with energy" I asked myself? The answer came subtly at first and then continued to get louder. "You need to stop eating all animal flesh, dead animals do not belong in your body!" It was weird. I'd always eaten meat. I thought all vegetarians were too skinny and undernourished. Plus, I tried being a vegetarian before and got very ill! Why now? The answer was even clearer. I didn't know what I knew about nutrition at the time. Just because I'd tried it previously didn't mean I'd fail again, it simply meant I can do it differently and succeed.

The real truth was that I couldn't continue to take the pain and suffering of animals into my body and not expect to experience pain as my body broke down and digested dead animal flesh. I'll leave you with a question … What are you really eating? Was it a happy chicken that skipped down to the barn who laid your eggs this morning or a happy pig that gave you your bacon? Or was it locked in a cage, force fed until it couldn't move, fed numerous amounts of antibiotics, ate the tails off other pigs, slaughtered and had its body dissected into hundreds of pieces for you to enjoy just one piece of bacon? For an idea on how animals really end up on your plate, check out either of these great documentaries *Food Inc.* or *Earthlings*.

Why am I so Stressed?

Thousands of years ago we suffered minimal amounts of stress. We lazily ate, slept on the earth/ground and basked in the sun. WOW! Has life changes or what? We now wake up to stress, the alarm clock goes and we wake up worried we're already running late. So, you throw breakfast down and rush off to work (it's barely even 8:30 and we've activated our fight or flight response). As humans we live in a society where it's necessary to function like this daily. We no longer have to run from a lion or sabre tooth tiger, yet we're exposed to one every single day. It's our daily stressful life. Our body has a primal need to run from stress, but we're running towards it by never giving our bodies a physical outlet. Yoga is a fantastic way to move these daily stresses out of our bodies, releasing them from the muscles and being able to restore peace to our mind at the same time. For you, you may not enjoy yoga and here's the best bit … you don't have to. It could be an evening walk, a run, lifting weights at the gym, any kind of physical activity. When you're going through a stressful period, that's the time to do a little more. Exercise releases endorphins, improves bone density and has so many other amazing benefits it's impossible to list them all here. Choose something that invigorates you and try to get 30 minutes in per day. You'll be amazed at how you feel.

Don't Drink The Kool Aide

Junk in. Junk out! If you were to put a chocolate bar and milk into the fuel tank of your car, it wouldn't really run very well. Why do we expect our bodies to run well when filled with pre-packaged products? If we did the same thing to our motor vehicle, we'd have to take it to the mechanics and clear the junk from our fuel tank. The same thing happens with our bodies and we must give it a break, allowing it to restore and reset. In the awe-inspiring documentary *Super Juice Me!* Jason Vale refers to this as the "Fish Bowl" process. Essentially, you have a fish bowl with clean water and various plants, providing all the nutrients for the fish. Now pour some refined white sugar, a load of fat, chemical dies and flavourings, cigarettes, beer, wine, bread, caffeine, ice-cream, a couple of cakes and some other 'food'. As you pollute this tank, the fish struggles to cope. After a little while, the fish becomes ill and experiences disease. Now try adding in a few medicines to help that fish get well and its body can't cope. It's important to know, all drugs are also poisons and all are toxic to the body in some degree (just consider the long list of side effects). How could a fish ever benefit from any medicine if its tank is full of toxic material? Clearly the whole reason WHY the fish became ill in the first place has never been treated. We need to clean the water in the tank. Juicing floods the body with nutrients, flooding the cells and bathing them. Within a 3-day period, you've begun to clean and clear all of the organs within your system. After 7 days, you've virtually cleansed all of your cells within your body and after 28 days, you've reset your body completely.

So here's a short checklist of my personal prescription for health:

- ✍ Meditate (30mins daily)
- ✍ Yoga (30 mins daily)
- ✍ Juice Fast Regularly (once per quarter)
- ✍ Eat Vegetarian/Mostly Vegan Diet (consisting of fresh fruits, vegetables, nuts and seeds and vegetable juices).
- ✍ Limit Caffeine and Alcohol

So where to start? Fire up your juicer! Make the juice recipe on the following page and watch one of the suggested documentaries.

Morning Magic Juice:
- 4 Carrots
- 1 Apple
- 6 Mandarins
- 1 knob Turmeric or Ginger

Place Turmeric through the juicer first, follow with mandarin, apple and carrot. Sit back, relax and enjoy the fabulous uplifting and anti-inflammatory properties.

Suggested watching:
- Fat, Sick and Nearly Dead
- Dying to Have Known
- Food, Inc.
- Earthlings
- Super Juice Me!
- The Gerson Miracle
- Food Matters

All of these documentaries can be found online at *FoodMattersTV.com*

Final Thoughts

The idea of health and dis-ease has become so overcomplicated and the majority of illnesses can be helped greatly by simply removing the rubbish from our diets and topping up our nutrient tank! What's so obvious to me now, wasn't at one time and I cannot believe how much I suffered in my early years. And, I think the reason I hadn't is possibly why most never do. I'd been conditioned from birth not to question the experts, especially when it comes to a life threatening illness like asthma (P.S. I still carry my blue inhaler as an emergency, even though I haven't used it for a number of years. It pays to be safe and I would never recommend not having medication for a life threatening illness). It is safe for you to question the information you see, hear and read! All of the answers are available to us and I'll end with a quote from famed Bio-Chemist and friend Danne Montague-King (Author of The Maybelline Prince)

 If you were not born with a condition, there's a high chance you can reverse it.

~ DANNE MONTAGUE-KING

Dedicated to YOU! Shall you enjoy everlasting health and happiness.

To all of my family and friends—I am filled with such gratitude for your love and support.

~ Damien Munro

Juliet Vorster

JULIET VORSTER is a global force for personal and planetary change. As an author, speaker, coach, counsellor, teacher, radio show host, and New Thought Minister, she is passionate about inspiring and empowering people to awaken to their essential worth and value, enabling them to live a thriving life.

Juliet has a home base by the Solent, on the south coast of England, from where she travels extensively. She serves as Treasurer on the Leadership Council for Centers for Spiritual Living, loves to walk on the beach, and feed donkeys in the New Forest. When she is not working, Juliet is passionate about singing and creating delicious, nutritious plant based food for friends and family.

Juliet@JulietVorster.com
www.JulietVorster.com

You're Better Than You Think You Are

Imagine how your life would differ if you believed in yourself totally. Imagine waking up tomorrow morning with no fear, no anxiety, no "I can't", no "what will they think". How would your life be if you could overcome overwhelm, master your mind and start living the life of your dreams? How would your life be if you owned your own power, trusted yourself, and never criticized yourself? How would you feel if you truly believed that you are the perfect you, capable of being and doing anything you want? Thousands of people around the world are already living that life because they have read and studied with many gurus and masters, or because they have had a profound mystical experience that delivered instant insight to the essence of who we each are. There are even some people who have been raised believing these things about themselves—I'm guessing, as you're reading this book, that's not you. It didn't use to be me either. I have arrived at this point through falling down, over and over again; each time, getting up and seeking more answers.

My name is Juliet Vorster, but that has not always been my name. In the first moments of my life I was given away by my mother. Initially I was placed into foster care, and about six weeks later I was adopted into my 'forever home' by the people I consider to be my parents. I didn't know it then, but this huge rejection planted a subconscious virus in my mind. It was programming that looked something like this:

> *Your mother (the one person in the entire universe who 'should' love and cherish you) gave you away; therefore, you must be totally unlovable and unworthy of love. Because you are unlovable people will always reject you and leave you. You are on your own and life will always be a struggle.*

Not exactly a direct pathway to a thriving life, I think you'll agree.

This virus worked really well. Over and over in my life I experienced rejection and struggle. Finally, in 2001, on September 11th, as the world trade towers were collapsing in the US, something inside me broke. It was like an over-stretched spring finally snapped inside me. I collapsed into a mental and emotional breakdown. I was 34 years old and my life was a total wreck. But, as Brené Brown says, "It wasn't a breakdown, it was a 'spiritual awakening'".

As I look back from my life now, I recognise my breakdown/spiritual awakening was the best thing that ever happened to me. We humans seem to grow most from adversity. What I have learned however, is that pain is not essential to growth. It is not compulsory to have a breakdown to achieve a breakthrough.

Even though I was at my darkest point, something within me knew that there had to be more to life, there had to be a different way of being. I started to reconnect to my inner knowing and in the long months during my recovery I returned to some of my earliest teachings. I re-read Louise Hay's excellent book 'You Can Heal Your Life', and this time I actually did the exercises. I started to meditate again, something I was first introduced to when I was sixteen. I took classes in stress management and work related stress. I attended groups and workshops wherever I could. As I reconnected to my inner knowing I allowed my intuition to guide me to different books, teachers, mentors, and guides of all kinds. Little did I know that something I was seeking for my own recovery would ultimately guide me to my life's purpose.

My recovery was by no means a quantum leap. I was out of the corporate world for almost two years. During this time, I was slowly starting to remember who I really was, and learning to like myself, just a little bit more than I ever had. I also learned huge amounts about how our minds work, the nature of reality, and how our minds and 'reality' interact.

What started as a way of gaining perspective and clarity in my own life became my journey into leading workshops, hosting radio shows, coaching, counselling and writing. If someone had told me back in the late 80s, as I left the Women's Royal Naval Service, that within twenty years I would be instructing, inspiring and motivating people globally to live a thriving life, I'm quite certain I would have thought they were completely bonkers. That's one of the reasons I'm so passionate about what I teach and practise. I know that if I can make these changes *anyone* can, and that includes you.

Life is a Journey, not a Destination

It wasn't a quantum leap; it was a vicious cat fight with me resisting almost all the way. Personal transformation is not for the faint of heart, it's for the courageous. The good news is that to create the changes you simply need to be willing to take the next step (whatever that may be). And here I am, living my thriving life, with no sign of the stress, anxiety and depression which led to my breakdown. I am able to look in the mirror and know that I'm okay. I get to spend every day inspiring, motivating and instructing people globally on how to live a life filled with purpose, passion, peace and love. I am truly blessed and deeply grateful for all the experiences (good and bad) that Life has brought to my door. If I hadn't had my breakdown, you probably wouldn't be reading this and I would still be working in the corporate sector. Life is good.

Skip the Four by Two and Get Started Now

I didn't achieve this transformation because I'm in any way special. What I have done can be repeated by anyone, including you. It doesn't matter what you have experienced before this moment. Regardless of what you have done, or had done to you, you can step beyond your programming, rewire your mind and your beliefs to embrace your thriving life.

Did I mention that it's not compulsory to have any form of breakdown to experience a breakthrough? It is, however, really useful to have a guide for how to rewire your mind, open your heart, and release the past. These things, and many others, are the building blocks that form the bridge from where you are, to where you want to be. For me, the first step was looking at my beliefs with gentle compassion. Let's begin.

Thriving is Your Birthright

If you are like me, this heading might be something of a newsflash. I did not grow up believing that I could achieve my dreams or live a life of my choosing. I was raised to believe that money didn't grow on trees, that I'd have to work hard, get a good education then work even harder to eventually make enough money to feel secure in my retirement. Does that sound familiar?

I was born into a belief system of survival. Neither of my parents had any experience of thriving in their lives, so they couldn't teach or model something they didn't know. When you think about your upbringing, what belief systems were being modelled and taught in your life? I invite you not to judge, simply allow a new awareness to unfold. None of us can teach something we don't know or understand. Your parents, caregivers and teachers were all doing the very best they knew how.

To get you thinking a little deeper, here are some specific areas of life to consider. What messages did you receive about:

- the differing roles of men and women
- the value of education
- the importance of healthy nutrition and exercise
- the value of money

- ✎ your own importance and value in the world
- ✎ how wealthy or poor people behave
- ✎ the need to work hard
- ✎ the importance of sticking at things and seeing them through
- ✎ your ability to make and keep money
- ✎ age/sexuality/skin colour/ethnic background/disabilities
- ✎ the importance of a good career, trade or profession
- ✎ using your imagination
- ✎ being different or standing out in some way

These are things that we bump into in everyday life. The chances are you will have opinions about each one. Those opinions are based on your belief system. It is really important not to judge yourself as good or bad for the beliefs, opinions and perceptions that you hold. Perhaps this is the first time you have consciously thought about what you believe. It may also be the first time you are considering where those beliefs came from, how they have affected you, and whether or not you want to continue buying into them.

As you become conscious of your beliefs and perceptions, you have an opportunity to evaluate them. Do this from a place of compassion, not a place of judgement. Your beliefs have got you to where you are today. Understanding and adjusting your beliefs is an essential step, if you want to change your life.

In evaluating your beliefs, here are some useful questions to ask yourself:

- ✎ Where did the beliefs come from? Are they actually yours, developed through your life experience, or have they come from others.
- ✎ Are they still true for you? Even if they were once your truth, if you haven't looked at them in a while, perhaps you have out grown them.
- ✎ How are the beliefs you hold serving and supporting your life today? Even if they are perfectly valid beliefs, if they are keeping you stuck in fear, doubt, self judgement, or any other state of being that doesn't contribute to a thriving life, perhaps it's time to release them.

As you spend time thinking more deeply about what you believe, and how those beliefs are playing out in your life, I encourage you to start writing down your thoughts. This is just for you; no one else will read it unless you let them. Writing things down will give you greater clarity, as well as helping you to make greater sense of the thoughts.

NOTE: If you have a belief that says something like, "I'm rubbish at writing, my handwriting is untidy, my spelling is awful and I don't have a clue about punctuation", just be gentle with yourself and notice if you resist my invitation to write down your thoughts. This could be one way your beliefs are holding you back.

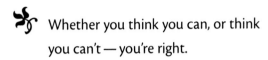 Whether you think you can, or think you can't — you're right.

~ HENRY FORD

Let this be the point in your life that you start thinking about what you think about. Once you become aware, then you can stop believing everything you think. Be willing to become more discerning about the thoughts, beliefs, and perceptions that you cultivate. Weed out those that don't serve or support your greatest dreams for your life. You deserve to live a thriving, abundant, joyous, vibrantly healthy life, filled with peace and love.

Here is a passage from my book, *Igniting Success Beyond Beliefs: How to get from where you are to your greatest yet to be*:

> "Just in case no one has ever told you before, here is the truth about you:
> *You are magnificent, you are beautiful, you are powerful, you are capable, you are brilliant and absolutely gorgeous. Your brain is just as powerful as everyone else's; you can achieve anything you want to. You are here, in your perfect, unique physical body suitcase to have fun, grow and thrive. Your presence on this planet is not some random accident, it is part of the fullness of Life. You are the place where the Infinite One becomes fully expressed in this finite world and you complete Creation. You are a radiant beacon of light and you are here to shine. If you weren't here, Life would be incomplete and the world a little dimmer.*
>
> This is true no matter what you have done or had done to you in your life. It doesn't matter if you can believe it about yourself or not, it is still true, and I hold that knowing for you until you awaken to it yourself."

This is the truth of your being. You are better than you think you are. You don't have to be defined by your history. In each and every moment you have a fresh opportunity to release the old thoughts and beliefs; embracing fresh possibilities that nourish and nurture your heart's desire.

It's important to be gentle with yourself as you start to become more aware of who you are, and who you're not. It is essential to remember that you are not broken, you don't need fixing, and that self-awareness builds the consciousness necessary to grow into an even greater expression of yourself.

We are all on this journey together. It's a journey of many twists, turns, peaks and troughs. As we travel, we are nudged, pushed, and guided to the perfect route for us, for now. The Knower with you knows what It's doing. Trust the process.

April L. Dodd, M.A.

APRIL L. DODD is an inspirational speaker, Executive Coach, compassionate life coach, award-winning actress, and author. With a master's degree in Spiritual Psychology, April serves as a trusted confidant, guide, and partner in co-creating transformational opportunities to rise above with thousands of children, professionals, and life enthusiasts. April resides in Chicago, IL, creating new possibilities to live every day to its fullest with Paul and their two children.

april@aprildodd.com
www.aprildodd.com

Rise

Imagine your beloved child shoved upon the playground, curled over as a fist bullets into their stomach. Imagine a boot driving into the back of your son or daughter's head. Imagine someone sitting on the swing set nearby and laughing at the scene of your bloodied child, and another person sitting close enough, who is capable enough, to save your child. You'd wish someone would "Bruce Lee" a few moves on the violators to save your most precious love. Well, I had a similarly unique spot on the playground that day.

I was sitting on the letter "M" of the alphabet squares that lined a popular park in the heart of Aspen's upscale pedestrian mall. I sat down next to my backpack, exhaled, and pulled out a bottle of water. My children and I had already exhausted ourselves touring the town by the time we got to the mall. As usual, it was crawling with a mix of tourist families and locals walking dogs, sipping cocktails at bistro tables outside sushi restaurants and cafes, or tossing dollar bills into the opened cases of Aspen Music Festival street violinists playing versions of Mozart or Coldplay, while children raced in and out of the intermittent fountain or scampered throughout the playground in the center of it all.

Hamilton had been more patient than a typical five-year-old to finally get there and unleash his energy around the sit-and-spin. Grace, his eight-year-old "Sissy Wissy" helped him spin at a controlled pace, so he wouldn't get too dizzy. I found a comfortable spot at the corner of the playground away from the affluent shoppers that strolled by, setting our heavy backpack of waters, snacks, and souvenirs down for a much-needed breather.

Now, I'm not an expert in karate. Nor am I an expert in parenting. But on this day I came close to using my high blue-belt on the playground, so I wouldn't have to ask myself the unsettling question that also has an unsettling answer: Why didn't I do anything?

"Mommy! Come on!" they yelled excitedly only seconds later from the crest of the first climbing rock. My children could not wait to conquer the attached rope bridge that reached the top of a huge boulder, "spidering" with other successful young climbers.

"Yeah, I'll be right there!" *Mommy just needs a breather first.* For the majority of this trip to Aspen, I'd had the kids consistently with me while my husband took his bike to mountain peaks, and his laptop and phone calls in the quiet library or coffee shops. While he managed high altitude and projects with skilled people, I managed high energy and emotional tantrums of little people. It gave me plenty of opportunity to practice the walking meditation and consciousness work I'd been doing with my spiritual teacher to keep myself centered and grounded in the present.

I needed this break. Not just from the overwhelm of solo parenting while on vacation, but also from the world's tragedies filtering the media, both social and visual. The shooting in Dallas of 15 white police officers the day before, inspired by the shooting by police of two African-American boys earlier that week, had me feeling off. I was not usually one to get involved in the news or politics, but it was all over the place and I was a tad shaken, as was much of the country. I'd taken a lot of quiet time recently to work with what my spiritual teacher and karate master had me doing daily: connecting and expanding the spirit that resides in me, to operate from this deep place inside instead of reacting to my children's and the world's dramas. That violence is *simply uncontained, unfocused, misdirected energy.* He'd also suggested I be mindful to watch my attachment to whatever I was getting from the drama and violence on the news, or it would feed my own chaos and fears. He was right. The recent killings had me a bit on edge for my family and my own mortality, which was already a trigger for me. For years I'd been carrying the heartache of one of my brothers who was randomly attacked and beaten, my other brother who barely survived a fall in a well, the aggressive cancer that stole both my parents before I was 39, and the most recent loss of my beautiful friend and mother-in-law who died suddenly during last year's trip to Aspen.

As I lifted my face toward the mountain sun, I took in a breath to connect myself with my inner spirit. I wanted to enjoy a long happy life with my kids and husband. I wanted to be so much for them … wanting to be the parent who tuned into the life of my kids, not to the lives of my Facebook friends whenever my kids scurried off. Facebook, as well as the news these days, had turned into a consistent negative focus of all the random instances of violence on innocent people. Because of this I'd gotten clear on two things: I love my children more than anything in the entire world, and it was time for me to clean up my own act and be an expression of peace, finding celebration through myself as a parent, a wife, a soulful spirit, and a citizen of this beautiful world.

It was at this moment that I saw teenage boys rustling about from the side of my eye, near the playscape upon which my children climbed. Then they stopped. Why were they on the playground anyway? Then they started again, wrestling aggressively this time. As I turned from my letter "M" seat, everything moved in slow motion as I saw the taller boy seize and pull a smaller boy to the ground, the taller landing purposefully on top of him to pin him down. Then, from another teen looming above with his eyes narrowed and teeth clenched, a fist came smashing on the small boy's face. Then another fist rifled into the boy's chest from another teen jumping with the opportunity to join in. And then I saw the fat kid, chambering back a kick that was headed straight forward into the upper back or head of the helpless boy on the bottom.

It's amazing that in an unexpected instance we can be faced with the decision to stand up or sit down, play it safe or fight for freedom, champion the greatest good or silence ourselves for safety. Am I going to sit here and wait for the highest good to happen, wait for someone else to step in? Do I stand by to help this poor boy or am I a bystander watching the attack unfold upon him?

My coaching audiences and children have heard me talk about how to give ourselves an important voice in this world, that the greatest gift we can give to others is to lift people up with it, not put them down, and here was a moment unfolding quickly in front of me.

At the same time, there were my kids only 10 ft away from possible danger.

So I found myself in a situation we never want to find ourselves in: watching violence happen when our intervention could make a difference, yet our children are near and could possibly be harmed as a result. Was I going to call for my children and scurry them away, turning their and my head to the victim of violence, brushing it off as nothing but "kids being kids" or "boys being boys" ... and while doing that send the message to "mind your own business," that this is appropriate behavior, that you can't make a difference anyway, and then stay awake throughout the night with shame and the dread that because I walked away, the victim might not have?

Or would I rise to be an advocate for this victim, standing all of my 5 ft 4 inches, 120 lbs to a group of violent preppy teenagers, who thought this was right, a rite of passage, even funny. Was I going to scurry my kids away to safety, or intervene to create safety for this victim and everyone else nearby?

In the last 2 months alone, I had been bombarded by the news reports of random acts of violence across our nation and globe, and of common people stepping in to take a stand against it. There were the three women enjoying a girl's night out in Santa

Monica, when they spotted a man at another table open a vial and put something into the drink of the woman he had known for a year and a half. As risky as they said they felt at first, they immediately notified the restaurant, as well as the woman, and hatched a brave plan that thwarted the whole potential rape and had the man arrested and charged for two felonies with $1 million bail. Then there was the newly-historical image burned in our nation's eyes: the unarmed 28-year-old black woman, Ieshia Evans, mother of a five-year-old, in a flowing dress who bravely stood calmly gazing down a row of heavily armed police officers in full riot gear in a Black Lives Matter protest following the shooting of African-American Alton Sterling. She apparently took part in the protest so she could 'look her son in the eyes to tell him she fought for his freedom and rights.'

But what burned most in my own eyes was the powerful image of my eight-year-old daughter, Grace. Only weeks before we were standing along the street of Aspen's annual fourth of July parade. Candy was being thrown from almost every vehicle, and kids were scrambling from the curbside, leaping in front of each other to get their share. A boy near us had already caught our attention when he was behaving rudely and disrespectfully to his mother, then to his father, then finally to his grandmother. Grace had noticed, too, but what really caught her attention was when her younger brother and other small children nearby were losing their share to the grabs and greedy snatches of this troublesome boy. Grace wasn't having any of it. She walked right up to this mini-bully, mid grab, and with as tall a stature as Iesha Evans stood, powerfully projected words upon this boy he'd apparently never heard. He froze, his smirk turned to an embarrassing frown, his eyes weakened. He dropped his candy, and his shoulders, and walked quietly away, ceasing to be a nuisance again that day. Grace lost neither her composure, nor her candy, but she did gain the experience that silence is a poor substitute for justice.

And as I watched these scenes play out in my family and on all sorts of media, I noticed one common thread that inspired me to want to rise up to be a part of it: The wild heart gets involved. It doesn't want to be on the sidelines. It's time to level the playing field. To we wild hearts, there is no more you vs. me, or us vs. them. It is WE. We get involved. We own this field. We own the game. These are the rules.

Now, for a moment before I acted, I didn't think about any guns that could have come out, and I didn't think I'd get that hurt if I did get physically involved (I have a few useful karate moves under my belt). I also realized that my children were safe up high on a playscape, and I knew that I was surrounded by a crowd of protective mothers and fathers who would intervene should I be immobilized in the act.

But the question I didn't consider was this: where were these people when the boy was first taken down? At any given moment there were at least 75-100 people in the immediate area to intervene, many of them closer than I was, many of them summer vacationing mothers and fathers of children also playing on the playground. What were they doing for the boy? What were they doing for me? Standing by, understandably protecting their own children, giving me the chance to rise up to be the change I wanted to see in the world instead of sitting by silent. That boy needed an advocate, if only for his absent mother by a mother who happened to be present. And that day it was me.

And who was I on this day? I was the small, blond, retired blue-belt in karate, tired mother of two, sitting there choosing to keep my eye on my kids instead of on my phone's Facebook app. I was the overwhelmed wife of a traveling and busy husband. The grieving daughter who'd lost both parents and a mother-in-law to sudden and violent illnesses.

Who was there that day? The me that had had enough. Enough of the daily news about attackers getting away with violence, the sneaky manipulation that betrayed the victims, victims who were people who could very easily be my own neighbor, or my family.

I remember the day I got a text message while on vacation in Texas that my brother, the one I consider my soul-mate of a brother, was randomly and savagely beaten, and left for dead in a ditch outside his quiet home in Rockford, Illinois. Though we stood up for each other growing up, and he always had my back, I grieved that I wasn't there to karate chop the man, to sweep the man's legs out from under him … pinning him down in a painful-if-he-moved shoulder twist, to protect my brother from the raging man's ruthless sucker punch to the nose that knocked my brother out, the neck grab that dragged him like a ragdoll to dump his unconscious body face first into a dirt-filled foxhole, the multiple boot kicks to his head.

And this is who I saw at the bottom of the pile on the playground that day, waiting for his head to get kicked in. And this is when I threw my water bottle aside, jumped up, and fiercely screamed "Hey!" over and over again, with every step I rushed upon them.

They stopped. The puncher ran. The older boy on top got up and sat on the wall, innocently. The boy on the bottom brushed himself off and sat next to him. The fat boy walked away, almost whistling coolly, but not without seeing me stare him down like a fiery mother bear.

What emerged from the very core of my being were intense admonishments fueled by a passion for peace like "you're a role model, this is ridiculous, that's hurtful, that's a human body, it's not yours to touch, that's violent, this is a community area, there are small children here, and they're watching YOU, if you want to act like that get out of here", and a soul guttural "NOW!"

Yet there was another me there that day. The one who has been taught that violence was an inside job and was simply unfocused, uncontained, misdirected energy.

And so, I became incredibly focused in that very moment, aware that I was being a powerful container of Spirit, speaking from the voice of a greater good, directing my energy not toward condemning them, but of holding them up to their greatest self, provoking them to step up because they could, or step away because they couldn't. Either way, this shit doesn't belong here, or anywhere, but your greatness does.

They stared at me, bewildered. I knew the kids all around were watching, too, especially my own, but I was unaware of the crowd, or the restaurants full of people sitting outside about 50 feet away who had stopped sipping and walking and were fixed on the whole situation.

The teen boys wiped themselves off and sat on the wall, their stereotypical personalities becoming more clear: the bully was "calm and collected," the victim scrawny but obedient still wanting to be liked by the leader, the sidekicks acting chill, including a laughing one, the fat boy punk, and the wimpy ones ran away.

I pointed fingers. "Are you ok?" I demanded from the victim sitting on the wall. Our eyes held in conversation for a moment. I saw his tears before he wiped them away. I wanted him to say, "No, I'm not," to let his face get wet as he unleashed the courageous words of personal defense, to let them fall from his lips and land straight between the eyes of his attackers. Instead he said, "Yes, I'm fine." I wasn't sure if he was saying yes, as in "yes, thank you ma'am, I'm not too hurt." Or yes, as in "I'm fine. This was nothing. Don't call me out as a wimp in front of them." His only power right now was to not speak up for the price of earning the respect of his friends. To hush himself so they were comfortable. "No you're not," I pushed on. "Your eyes are red, and this is NOT what friends do to each other. You're better than this!"

The laughing kid looked like a hyena, hat off to the side with messy hair sticking out, and a strange laugh as he just watched from the hammock.

"I still think it's funny," he fumbled.

"I know you do. You're part of the problem," I retorted as I approached him. He continued to laugh. I glared at him, one breath away from saying, "Grab my wrist. I dare you." A simple grab of my wrist and I could have twisted his arm into a painful karate position in seconds. Just to see this twerp crippled to the ground, helpless, pleading, would have made everyone's day. I narrowed my eyes at him instead. Violence begets violence. "Get out of here, NOW, or I'll call the police!"

I had done my part. This kid, this victim, however, was bullied into silence. Bullied into a definition of himself that was louder than the small voice inside his little body. This definition was the enemy of his freedom ... betraying the world where he desperately wanted to exist ... betraying himself alone.

The boy who was beating him up, the apparent leader, pushed his dark sunglasses closer to his face as he made himself casually comfortable next to his victim. "We get it," he said coolly, leaning closer into the kid, as if they were united buddies.

"What!?!" I demanded, as if he was talking back.

"We get it," he repeated, with a slow lifting of his jaw.

"Good!" I barked, and began to walk away. But his words halted me in my tracks. He was too calm; it was almost creepy. I didn't trust it. Yet, the first thing that came to mind were the flashes of times my own husband has said this to me. I suddenly doubted myself. Did I overdo it? Was I too harsh? Did I overstep my bounds, or misread this situation? He said it so calmly, almost chillingly calm. It was time for me to stop. Was I acting out from what my teachers had taught me about my own unhealed "inner terrorist"?

Along with being taught that violence was "simply unfocused, uncontained, misdirected energy," I knew it best not to waste my time pointing fingers. Instead, the most important and empowering thing I knew I could do would be to focus on healing my own inner violence to myself, the kind that looked like beating up myself or my children with cruel judgments that crept out in the ways I parented and managed my own life experiences. And since what goes on inside of us all is what we create outside of us, my responsibility alone is to raise my consciousness and that of my children to what's going on inside so we can meet the outside as an active participant of loving compassion.

Does this solve the world's problems? No, but I am raising little beings that for now feed off of me and whatever I have consumed, be it food or thought. One day soon they will act independent of me, seeking out their own consumption of many kinds in order to live and thrive, most likely it will be what's similar and common to what I gave them. My negative attitude pollutes my and their consciousness, feeding them with a poison of "againstness." My job is to remove the barriers to my own inner peace so that I may provide fertile ground from which my children, and any others I may come in contact with, may thrive and contribute to creating, maintaining, and participating in a peaceful world.

The problem with this practice of looking within is that it removes the ability to take anything personally. It forces us to look at violence neutrally, and even more threatening, it forces us to not make it about us, after all, it was just unfocused, uncontained, misdirected energy. Everyone has done that before. It thus leaves us to look at our own personal triggers that are keeping us from looking at the situation without the energy of hurt and anger, and to look within at what judgments we still hold upon ourselves. It removes the personal judgments we hold, and forces us to look at what the barriers are to creating focused, contained, and positively-directed solutions within the situation, within ourselves, within our families, within our world.

But we don't typically live there. We live in the duality of a good/bad, you/me, victim/persecutor mentality. We separate. We don't embrace the results of our own participation in this kind of land. Instead we fight against it, turn away, point fingers, or pretend it never happened.

It's conditioned, it's fed throughout our life's experiences, it's habitual, it's familiar. It's standing on the sidelines of life, hoping something else will happen. And we all know that hope is not a strategy. And we all know that life doesn't happen to us. We create it by the way we participate with it.

The question then is this: Who is willing and able to take action, to have enough courage to make a shift: an inner shift to heal our own internal suffering, and thus to be a force in these times to end outer suffering? Who will get involved? Who will participate, not in the luxury of duality's division into you and me, but who will become an active, conscious participant in the Oneness of We?

To take a stand does not mean to stand divided, to pick sides, to be against. It simply means to place one's feet firmly in this moment, and rise up to participate with the all of now. What does that mean? It means that we get involved, that our waking up is an invitation for others to wake up, too. That we jump into this life, this moment, this situation from a place of deep connection and knowing that comes from love, from the focus of One.

And sometimes that looks like being a mom on a playground, not hiding as the bystander, but instead speaking as the power of the wild heart. What if we were able to speak up from a place of powerful compassion, of seeing the loving being behind the scene, of representing the creator of greatness within them? What if we were able to speak to this, to them, to hold this out for them to step into? It takes every bit of our energy to be contained in one place to not leak out all over the place and attack, run, or freeze. It takes focused attention on the pulse of the truer truth within each of us. And from here we can direct our energy toward something higher.

If it doesn't matter to you whether you stand up or stand by, then you cannot know what it feels like to walk along your own country driveway to assist a lost driver and have your face punched to a bloody pulp, being dragged by your throat and thrown face down into a ditch, head smashed in by steel toe boots, unable to move or call for help for 30 minutes while your brain swells, and blood drips into your throat as you desperately gasp to breath, not knowing if another breath will arrive, or even help. There was no one there to help my brother. And every day he is reminded of this. And so am I.

I walked away from the teens, the crowd began to disperse, and the boys started leaving. A mom with an 18 month-old walked up to thank me, she said she saw what was happening and "wanted to stop it, too." I knew she couldn't have done anything. She'd likely have to leave her baby unsafe in order to do so. I would've chosen the same if I were her.

Hamilton ran to me from the climbing bridge. "Mommy, I saw you talk to those boys." He looked troubled. "Did you?" I got concerned that I had gone overboard. Had I been a good role model? Or did I just lose my cool? I knew that kid needed to be saved, but had I been extreme? "What did you think about that?" I asked. Always my little lover, he hugged me and said, "You did good, Mommy. I love you," and ran into the field.

The fat boy, the runner, and the laugher came around the corner, almost celebrating, "Did you see him? Ha! Did you hear her say …"? Then they saw me staring at them and immediately stopped laughing, lowering their heads only a little as they smirked and walked away to some nearby tables.

As I went into the field to meet Grace and Hamilton, who were now running toward the sprinklers, a wealthy-looking older woman with what may have been her elementary school grandson came to find me. "My husband and I saw what happened from the restaurant. We are both doctors and have seen these things turn into serious brain injuries. Thank you for what you did. Just thank you." As she turned to go, Grace squeezed my hand and shouted, "Yay, Mommy! You did it!" I put my finger to my lips with a smile. I didn't want the attention or to be thanked. This wasn't about me.

If we are going to be bystanders to moments in front of us that call forth our wild heart, amidst the mess of the hurt that is unfolding in excruciating ways across our nation, we'd best be committed to sleeping with the one question everyone always asks, "Why didn't I say or do anything?" … saying goodnight to a moon that also rises upon the soul whose life may have forever been impacted by our choice to walk away. If we can rise up in our fierce loving, we can trounce the hatred and offer hope to what once seemed powerless. We can intervene and make a positive difference.

And here's the best part. We already know this. We've all had experiences that have taught us the powerful impact of our stepping in, stepping up, or standing by. If we can stay grounded as a conscious active participant for what is true, what is love, and what is right, then together we can make our children and our playgrounds the safe and peaceful expressions of love and life they should be.

To my lovely daughter, Grace. You are a divine inspiration to me, and in this world. I love you more than words, always, in all ways, no matter what, forever.

To my brother, Jim, for your fierce determination to stand up for your own life, while blessing mine at the same time.

To every being that has ever courageously brought light to the dark places in ourselves, in others, or in the world, and thus answered the cry to come home to what's essential: Love.

April L. Dodd

Lowell Gillespie

LOWELL GILLESPIE, born on January 1, 1945 has lived almost all his life on the same central Illinois farm having many cherished experiences as the world forever changed around him. He is now a 71-year retired farmer (30 Years), retired Eastern Illinois University Employee (31 years: Building Service Worker 15 Years and Steam Plant Operating Engineer 16 years), and a retired Army National Guardsman (20 Years). He worked at these three occupations simultaneously while helping raise four wonderful children with his fabulous wife and best friend, Judy. During this time, he was also a youth director, Sunday School teacher, Sunday School Superintendent, Lay leader, 4-H leader, and FFA Councilman. After he retired at age 56 he took a Hospice training course and was trained as a Steven Minister who is a person who listens to people talk through their problems. He loves to write poetry writing about what's going on around him. The shortest poem he wrote is called

No Poet: *I'll make it brief. I hear it is your belief that you think I'm a poet. You can be sure that if I were, I would not try to show it.*

Pieces of the Puzzle

My six-year-old grandson and I planted potatoes four months ago on Good Friday. Last week we went out to the garden to dig enough potatoes to fill a bushel basket. A plentiful return for our effort in the Spring. If we would have not planted those seed potatoes in the Spring, we would have no potatoes to dig up. The seed *potatoes* must be placed into top quality soil with all the necessary nutrients for the plant to thrive. We placed four inches of composed leaves on top of the seed potatoes to keep the moisture in the ground and discourage the weeds from growing.

In the same way a plant needs good soil for a good start to grow properly and precautions taken to assure weeds won't choke it out, a family needs a good spiritual foundation to developed into a productive unit. If we allow God's virtues of *love, joy, peace, patience, kindness, goodness, gentleness and self-control (Galation 5:22 NIV)* to become our own we can keep out the predators that destroy our lives including *sexual immorality, impurity and debauchery, idolatry and witchcraft, hatred, discord, jealousy, fits of rage, selfish ambition, ... (Galations 5:19 NIV)*

Wow! Wouldn't it be good if I could keep all of those predators away from myself and my family? I'll admit I have struggled with some of these while trying to raise our family. When I try to do the right things, I find myself messing things up. I know if I look to God, he will show me a way out of my self-made predicaments. I love the way God uses those around me to help me through these difficult times.

One of the traditions my wife and I started the first day we were married was saying grace before every meal. After the kids started coming we also had devotions before our evening meal. I would read to them from the Bible and explain what it meant. These sessions kept getting longer until the kids started losing interest. *Oh my, what have I done?* My wife came to the rescue when she started reading *The Little House on the Prairie* series of books by Laura Ingalls Wilder. Our children loved listening to their mother read. The contents of those books taught them the Christian values that I was trying to teach them from the Bible. *Thank you, Judy!*

I found myself getting involved in too many activities instead of taking care of the family. Besides working at the steam plant of the local university, I also farmed raising corn, wheat and hay; cared for a small herd of beef cows; and custom baled hay. Serving in the Illinois National Guard kept me busy one weekend a month, plus I attended a weekly prayer meeting where I stayed until almost midnight. I loved my family and wanted the time to be with them so something had to give.

We decided to leave the church where we were the youth leaders and I was the Sunday School Superintendent, so I could devote what spare time I had to help with the family. We found a church that we liked where there were kids the same ages as ours so they would feel more comfortable. Soon after we arrived, we found out they needed new youth directors, so of course we had to help them out. We found ourselves in the same situation as we were before. More and more teenagers kept coming to the youth meetings where we were teaching them how to follow Christ and allowing Him to be their personal savior. Three of our own children accepted the Lord while attending this church. We had the youth group for about three years before vacating that position.

Shortly after exiting the youth director position, I soon got involved with the bus ministry at the same church. I would go out on Saturday mornings after working all night at the local university recruiting kids to ride a bus to church on Sunday morning. I got up early on Sunday morning to ride the bus picking up the kids and then taking them home after church. After coming home one Saturday afternoon, Judy met me at the door and told me our oldest son had been bouncing a ball all day on the only piece of concrete we had because he could find nothing else to do. I gave up the bus ministry so I could help take care of our family. I was doing what I thought was good at the time but I was taxing my health and neglecting the family God had given me to help raise.

The farm was a good place to raise our family. I loved the way things worked out when we decided to install a wood stove in the corner of our living room. This endeavor gave us many enjoyable days in the woods as a family unit cutting, splitting, stacking, and carrying in wood. Another muscle building enterprise for the family was baling hay every summer. Using friends and neighborhood teenagers, we would cut, rake and bale hay on several different farms throughout our small community. The hay bales weighed sixty to seventy pounds each and were first stacked on a wagon by two people with another person driving the tractor. The hay was unloaded from the wagon into our neighbor's barns to feed their horses and cows with another three to four-person crew. Each of our own children took their turn on the hay baling crews. We paid them just like we did the other employees. A good work ethic was built into all four children as they helped out around the farm.

On April 1st of one year, our youngest daughter came into the house after feeding her goats to tell us one of her nanny goats had just given birth to twins. We did not believe her since it was April Fool's Day. She said, *Really, there are two baby goats out in the pen. Come on out and see for yourself!* Sure enough, there were two kids standing on wobbly legs getting their first taste of momma's milk. Since one of them was a male, she stated, *I'm going to take this goat to the Coles County 4-H Show next year, win Grand Champion Market Goat, then take him it to the slaughter house where they can make goat burgers out of him so we can eat him.* Everything happened just like she said it would. She learned early on that following through with her goals was very beneficial and rewarding.

When she became old enough to drive, she and some of her friends gathered in front of their favorite restaurant. A young man drove up on his brand new motorcycle and asked if anyone wanted to take a ride. My daughter and one of her friends squabbled over who would take the first ride with him on his shiny pride and joy. My daughter won the squabble, but before she jumped on the back of the motorcycle her friend held out her newly purchased leather jacket for her to wear. She slid her arms into the soft suede sleeves of the borrowed jacket and hopped on the seat behind the young man just before they sped off on the first ride of what he hoped to be many rides of the evening. Zipping down Fourth Street past the Wesley United Methodist Church, they rounded the curve that lead out of town and charged off toward Lincoln Log Cabin. Turning around before reaching their destination, they rocketed back toward town. As they tried maneuvering around the Fourth Street curve at the edge of the city, the bike skidded on some loose gravel throwing both of them off the newly purchased bike. Our daughter's head slammed against the hard surface of the road. The soft leather jacket was lacerated as she slid across the asphalt. The young man driving the bike was not hurt. Fortunately, a fellow classmate and her boyfriend drove upon the scene shortly after it happened. Her boyfriend went for help while the classmate held my daughter's head up out of the water filled ditch until the paramedics arrived.

We rushed to the hospital emergency room as soon as we heard the news, arriving shortly after they brought her in. Many of her friends were crowded in the waiting room praying for her. I ran back and forth from her room to her friends informing them of her condition. She suffered a severe concussion from hitting the hard asphalt but not a scratch was found on the rest of her body. The leather jacket saved her from further injury and might have even saved her life. The doctors decided to transfer her up to another hospital 50 miles away where they were better equipped to treat head injuries.

When she arrived, they packed her whole body in ice to keep her head from swelling and put her in a coma so she would not move. Her brain had bounced around in her head when it hit the pavement. They kept her in a coma for a week. We would take turns sitting with her, telling her how much we loved her. One of her brothers read books to her during his time. As she was coming out of the coma she started saying random numbers which no one could figure out why. We finally looked up to where she was pointing on the wall and saw numbers scrolling across a screen.

Her oldest brother (the guardian angel) came home from his Naval ship off the coast of California to be with her during her recovery. Since he was used to being up during the nighttime hours, he took the graveyard shift to keep an eye on her. One night she decided she had to go to the bathroom, so she slipped out of bed without setting off the bed alarms nor waking up her brother. When he noticed she was gone, he panicked: he had shirked his duty. Relief came to him when she came out of the bathroom and hopped back into bed.

From the very beginning of this tragic ordeal, my wife and I had an unexplainable heavenly peace come over us. We both knew that whatever happened to her was okay. We knew that God was in control. This comforting peace was reinforced as friends and family came to pray with us and spend time with us. The young man who was driving the motorcycle was very perplexed. He came to the hospital several times to see how she was doing and told us over and over how sorry he was about the accident. My wife and I had every reason to be angry at him, but we were not. We did everything we could to comfort him and assure him we forgave him completely. He just could not understand why we were not upset with him. God's ways are higher than man's ways.

Our daughter was in rehab for several weeks after her accident learning how to walk and talk again. My wife and I made the fifty mile trip up to be with her every day. Her sister stopped in to give her HOPE. Her brother, closest in age, went up and read to her as much as he could between his collegiate classes.

The father of the friend who lent her the leather jacket, organized a fundraiser night to raise money for our extra expenses we entailed during our daughter's recovery from her accident. A large number of people attended the event. Since she was still in rehab in an unstable and dazed condition, her mother went to the event to thank everyone for their love and support.

When she finally came home for good, she had missed out on so much school that we arranged a tutor for her so she could complete her junior year of school which continued well into the summer. Her classmates and friends were astonished to see her walking and talking again when she walked through the door for her senior year of high school. The school administrators would not let her back on the varsity cheerleading squad because they did not want to be liable for any further injuries she might receive while performing her cheerleading routines. This hurt her almost as much as the accident. After she graduated from high school she got accepted at the local university and immediately tried out and made the Freshmen Cheerleading Team. Our family is tough! The lasting difficulties of her accident were her loss of smell, frequent headaches, confusion and depression. FAITH, HOPE, and LOVE brought us all through this nightmare.

When this same daughter was attending the hometown university she got involved in the student government and ran for student body president. Some of the students that were opposing her threatened her life and made it so stressful for her that she dropped out of school. Shortly after removing herself from the stress she was in, she decided she would finish her education at a school out of state where a professor that was referred to her by her personal psychologist taught. She wanted to leave immediately. I told her she was not leaving without having a place to stay when she got down there. She made some calls and had a place to stay that very same day.

We helped her pack what she could into her old beat up mini station wagon and off she went on her seven-hour journey. Knowing that she would need a job to support herself she stopped at chain restaurant close to where she would be living. As she opened the door to the restaurant she was greeted by a young waiter who ask if he could help her. When she told him she was looking for employment he said he would take her to the manager. On the way he asked,

"What is your name?"
"Katina Gillespie"
"Where are you from?"
"Charleston, Illinois"
"Do you know Lowell Gillespie?"
"He is my dad."
"While going to National Guard meetings with your dad, I attended the church services he was presiding over each month. If it weren't for your dad, I would not be a Christian today."

Distraught by the circumstances life threw at her, she had her FAITH and HOPE renewed when she found God's loving presence had gone before her to prepare the way. A small world and a big God.

Another family event happened in 2012 while I was exercising at the University's gym where a nurse watches over the heart patients that choose to go there at 5:30 in the morning. The nurse noticed my draggy behavior was becoming too much for me to handle and my EKG showed signs of more heart problems. I was sent via ambulance to the local hospital, then transferred up to the Heart Institute 50 miles north. The doctors decided it was necessary to open my chest up again so they could perform a CABG Redu which meant they would replace two of the three bypasses I had back in 1998 during my first open heart surgery. This procedure was scheduled for the following week so the family had time to come home. Their thoughtfulness and kindness was a very uplifting time for me. My oldest son, Michael Lowell (*the ARCH ANGEL / ESCORTING ANGEL*) drove over from Indianapolis. My oldest daughter, Kimberly HOPE, living close by, was with her mother during the heart cath. My younger son Matthew Charles, our *AMBASSADOR* traveled all the way from Hong Kong and Katina FAITH, the youngest, flew in from Florida. They joined my wife, Judy (*THE STRONG ONE*), who was always by my side holding me up with her loving presence. Our two nieces Tammy and Sherri (only daughters of my two older brothers) also came to join us. They all played an important role in my survival of my second heart surgery.

We all participated in some very special family time activities a day before my surgery. Since there were trees down in the front yard from a new road being built, the family decided to clean up the debris with the sit down supervisor watching from his lawn chair and 2-year-old grandson sitting on his lap. Mike ran the chain saw while the rest of them loaded up the small limbs in my 2500 Chevrolet Silverado pick-up truck. Matthew drove the truck considering he had not driven a vehicle for several years since he had moved to Hong Kong. Tammy and Sherri took turns driving my 30 horse Kabota loader tractor hauling the burnable chunks of wood down the road to the farm house on the other side of the creek. They had never driven a tractor before.

After the trees were cleaned up we all gathered for a tour of the farm house where I grew up. We had pictures taken in the basement in front of an old coal bin door and also right outside the small back door of the white house. Back at our house, all of us continued working late into the night on a Chinese puzzle that Matthew had brought from Hong Kong. We put the last piece of the puzzle in place one minute before we went out the door to go to the hospital. All the pieces were fitting together for a successful operation and quick recovery. Any temptation of negative thinking about the outcome of this second heart surgery had been wiped out with the love and presence of the people God had placed in my life. These people are called family.

The following is a humbling post we received on Facebook two years ago from our son Matthew as he was riding the train up to Chicago to catch his flight back to Hong Kong where he teaches English through music and drama:

Every time I come home for a visit, the number of days I am actually here are longer, but the time seems to fly faster and faster. I am not sure if that is a sign of aging or nostalgia pushing things along or if time is actually moving faster, but it certainly is never long enough. There are so many things I wish I could express, but there aren't really words poetic enough. I have come to realize ever more how extremely blessed I am to have been born into the family I was. We are all so diverse—we couldn't be more different as individuals — but at its core, our family has an intense love for one another and compassion for all people. This is most assuredly because of 2 truly amazing human beings, Lowell and Judy Gillespie. Two people who, even when they have had very little, made sure everyone around them had enough. They provided an example of what it means to sacrifice for others as they taught us that the greatest gifts are from the heart and can't be bought. A Mother of everyone who passed through her door, who cannot stop taking caring of the smallest detail even when she has long earned her rest, A Father who continues to mentor and guide and share such great joy. Thanks Ma and Pa. I am who I am today because of all you have given. You are truly the most 'special' of all.

We are all family and all need each other as we pass through this life. These few illustrations from our family's life show how we can all overcome the struggles that come our way with FAITH in God and in ourselves to give us HOPE for the future knowing that LOVE will always prevail.

I would like to dedicate this story to my wife, Judy, who has been the stronghold of my life for 50 wonderful years. She understands me more than I understand myself. So calm and steady, always looking for ways to help out. Gently rebuking me when I need it and encouraging me when I need lifted up. We have found that we should never put each other down, not even in jest, for we both get hurt too easily. Thank you for being my best friend.

- Lowell Gillespie

Tammy Goodspeed

TAMMY GOODSPEED is a Mental Health Therapist at a Community Hospital in Kokomo, Indiana. She holds a Bachelor's in Psychology from University of Illinois and a Master's in Pastoral Counseling from Lincoln Christian University. Early in her career, she worked with troubled youth in California and Indiana and as a Crisis Therapist at a Mental Health Hospital in Indiana. After seeing so much brokenness in the lives of precious young people, Tammy devoted the next 15 years to her children as a stay at home mom, determined that her children would never doubt a day in their lives how much they are loved. During this time Tammy served as a Voluntary Youth Leader as well as a volunteer counselor for United Way. She has a passion for young people, for those who are hurting, and is dedicated to encouraging others as they transform from brokenness to peace.

Beautifully Broken

Broken and Ugly (or so I once thought)

I will never forget some of my first deeply broken moments. The first one happened my senior year of high school. I remember sitting in French class with my heart breaking after my first love-my high school sweetheart of 3 ½ years-broke up with me for the final time. I sat there at my desk with tears streaming down my face unable to focus on anything but the feeling that I hurt so deeply it felt as if my heart would stop forever. In that moment Madame glared at me from the front of class and said in a callous tone, "What's wrong with you? This isn't the time for that." I held my breath as I tried to stop the tears from flowing but was unable to. Madame then pointed her finger at me with no empathy whatsoever and gestured for me to leave. I was sent to the principal's office and was yelled at for not paying attention in class. I never understood why people did not even try to understand my pain. Nobody even asked why I was hurting. I was sent back to class and once again I tried my best to focus. I remember sitting with headphones on in my booth listening to French-English dictation. All I heard was my own thoughts in my head. I wondered why I was not good enough. I wondered why I was unlovable. It simply did not occur to me that I was perfectly lovable just the way I was. It did not occur to me that often the flaw is in the other person due to their inability to find the beautiful in broken things. I certainly did not know that this would someday become one of my greatest gifts out of which I operate.

It would also be many years before I would learn to love myself. In that moment I did not know that I was not defined by someone else's rejection. I tried to fill the void in my life looking for love and acceptance. I entered a downward spiral of self-destruction in attempt to drown my pain with alcohol and guys. One mistake led to another. By the ripe young age of 21 I was married and divorced (all within the same year). Once again I was left broken and feeling absolutely unlovable. This time I had nobody to blame but myself. I was living with the consequences of my actions. My mom once told me I was like Dr. Jekyll and Mr. Hyde when I drank. I would often hear my mom's voice echo in my head reciting her version of the famous words by Henry Wadsworth Longfellow;

> *"the little red-haired girl with a curl in the middle of her forehead," she would say, "when she was good, she was very good indeed, but when she was bad, she was horrid."*

The day my husband left me, I called my father, unable to speak. He heard my cracked voice on the phone and knew just what I needed. He told me, "Honey I love you no matter what mistakes you have made. I will always be here for you. I will always believe in you." He then directed me to go directly to my very first Alcoholics Anonymous meeting where he arranged to have someone he knew meet me. Admitting I was broken was the first step towards my upward climb of putting back the pieces of my life.

The problem with making bad choices, is that it results in losing the trust of others. I lost trust of my close family except for my father but he did not live nearby so I was unable to lean on him. I remember one time when I saw the disappointment in my family's eyes and it felt so difficult to find any hope for myself. I walked over to my best friend's mom's house and she responded to me with the unconditional love I needed. I lay with my head on her lap as she comforted me and told me she believed in me. I know that I needed to hear those words that day. I have never forgotten the love of her maternal heart that comforted me in that moment and gave me hope to go on another day.

I cannot tell my story without mentioning the love of one of the kindest souls I have ever known, my Uncle Lowell. I grew up enjoying our special trips to grandma's house at the farm. My aunt and uncle lived just across the creek and were always a part of our family gatherings. My best friends were my cousins. I was the city mouse, my cousin closest in age to me was the country mouse. She was the good one and I was the naughty one. I counted the days to visit my country cousins. During my escapades on the farm I often found a few ways to get us into trouble. I was scolded when I deserved it but never without my uncle's gentle grace as he reminded me I was still loved even when I messed up.

After my life fell apart, I had such a hard time accepting grace. How could I be lovable if I made so many mistakes? Yet Uncle Lowell believed in me always and often told me so. He reminded me that my story was not over yet. He told me he saw a beautiful future for me and that I just needed to reach for it and never give up working towards my dreams. His words gave me strength to do just that. I completed my Bachelor's in Psychology from University of Illinois at the end of that year. I fell off the wagon for one short month then got back on track. I went on to achieve my Master's degree in Counseling from Lincoln Christian University. I married a good man and have three beautiful daughters. I went on to serve as a volunteer Youth Leader at various churches for twenty-two years. I stayed home for fifteen years to raise my children and worked as a volunteer counselor for United Way for five of those years. I am still sober today, 27 years later. I never would have believed any of this would have been possible if it were not for those who loved me in my brokenness. Somehow in my brokenness they saw the beautiful that I could become. Today I spend my life loving the broken and helping others learn to love themselves, as I encourage them to start over, and keep moving forward. I am so blessed to go to work every day to do what I love.

Who are the Broken?

Some people find messed up people annoying. I find them beautiful. Not because I love drama (I don't). I love the soul, which is imperfect. I am not talking about romantic love. I am talking about agape love. I am referring to the human ability to care for a person, to want what is best for them, and to wish them no evil.

Who are the broken? It is the teacher, the school principal, the executive, the blue collar worker, the bully, the victim, the chronically ill, the widow, the pastor's wife, the pastor's kid, the pastor, the teenager, the brother in midlife crisis, the janitor, the lawyer, the doctor, the man who stands in the meal line, the one who serves at the mission, the neglected child, the single mom who does whatever it takes to get by, but it is still not enough. It's the one who seems perfect on the outside, but is messed-up on the inside. It is me. It is you. It is all of us.

Those of us who are really honest with ourselves know that we are not perfect. We would like others to believe we are. But the truth is nobody this side of heaven is perfect. Not one. I don't know about you but just when I overcome one flaw I seem to find another shortcoming that I want to overcome. I have grown to embrace my flaws as a challenge. I have come to realize that my flaws and struggles are part of my story which make me who I am and give me the heart and compassion to love others. I love broken people! Why? Because broken people are real. People who shed tears peel back the plastic layers to reveal the beautiful soul within.

The M&M's

When I was in my early twenties, I worked as a Mental Health Tech at a group home in Azusa California. Two years later I worked at a group home in Indiana. Both of these homes had one thing in common: tough kids with broken lives. The home in

Azusa was run by a former gang member from downtown Compton. Many of our kids were boys who grew up in homes with no father. They were children who never knew anyone over the age of 30 who was not in jail or dead. Some of these boys were victims of sexual abuse. Some of them abused others. Some participated in drive-by shootings as a rite of passage into the group who would forever get their back. Gang activity was a way of survival. The tough exterior of these kids was the face the world saw. But I was blessed with special moments where I was able to break past that tough exterior to get a glimpse of the sweet kid underneath. It was then that I realized that broken people were like M&M's. These tough kids may have seemed cold and hard on the outside but they were soft and sweet on the inside. They were just like any other kid who needed to be seen for who they really are deep inside and to be loved unconditionally in spite of their flaws.

Tilted Halos

I spent 22 years of my life as a volunteer youth leader. It did not take long for me to discover that the church kids were just as broken as the gang kids. I helped mentor other leaders, as I taught them to touch people's lives with love and hope. Our Youth Group welcomed the kids who grew up in church with hidden problems. We welcomed the kid who was rough on the outside that other Youth Groups rejected. We listened to their stories and together we cried, prayed, and shared joy as people began to heal. Some of the most beautiful moments happened during my days as a youth leader. For it was there that I embraced the term 'Beautifully Broken'. It was so easy to love those kids in their brokenness. It was then that it dawned on me that my brokenness was not ugly. It is in that broken place that true healing begins. A healthier perspective changed the way I looked at mistakes in myself. I was able to understand that every time I mess up I have to be perfectly broken in order for the pieces to be put back together. The mended life then becomes a priceless mosaic even more beautiful than the original. It is in these moments that life transforms with character that is unique and like no other.

But How???

Normally, I can love people. I have a high tolerance for annoying behavior because I can see the hurt that is underneath the behavior. My husband once told me I have always had an extraordinary sense of compassion towards others. I used to wonder why others could not do the same until he pointed out to me it is uncommon.

Over the years, I have had many people ask me how I am able to love the broken. How do I love the one that gets on people's nerves? How do I love the annoying one or the one who has hurt me? First of all, I think the love in me was planted there by the love of God. In my darkest hours God loved me even when I was unlovable. One night as I wrestled with guilt and feelings of unworthiness I cried out to God, "I am so messed up. I am so unlovable. Will you still love me if I'm imperfect?" Immediately, I sensed comforting words of the Holy Spirit whisper to my soul saying, "In your brokenness I will love you perfectly. I want to be with you in your brokenness, to love you as you are ... until you learn to love yourself." I was loved even when unworthy of love. I have so much gratitude in my heart for that. I am forever grateful for the people in my life who manifested God's love through their words, comfort, and belief in me. My life was forever changed because of them. It was because of unconditional love that I learned to love myself and love others.

The key to loving unconditionally is found in two places. First you must look inside your heart. Remind yourself you are not perfect either. It is very easy to notice the things we do not like about others. Unfortunately, many people "throw out the baby with the bathwater" once the ugly surfaces. I believe there is enough ugly in every one of us to make any of us qualify as 'flawed' or seemingly unlovable. I don't know about you but I don't want to be discarded the minute someone discovers one of my flaws or the day I make a mistake or disappoint someone. I guarantee that I am not perfect and will certainly mess up at some point. Just as I do not wish to be rejected, and I believe it is equally important not to give up on others.

The second key is to look deeper, past the hard outer shell, to discover the place where the tender broken pieces dwell within the other person. When someone's flaws become evident, don't give up on them. Look for the one thing you can appreciate, respect, admire, love, or have compassion for ... and build from that. I believe that everyone-even the worst of us are lovable if you look for the soft sweet center.

A wise professor once taught me that Eastern cultures have a more realistic perspective of life. The essence of love and life is not all black or white. It is not all good or all bad. Look at the yin and yang. It Is a perfect balance of dark and light; a synchronicity of two opposite forces that work together to form a whole. People are not all good or all bad. We are both.

I was once challenged. When I was 24 years old I worked with a small group of people during my internship. One of the men always seemed to have sarcastic comments directed at me. He was annoyed with me and sent off the vibe that he did not like me for no apparent reason. Near the end of the internship it came out during a small group session that he did not like redheads because he had a bad past experience with a redhead. He transferred these feelings onto me and treated me with unmerited disregard. This was at a time in my life when I cared very much what people thought of me. I internalized it. I did not know at the time how to have peace or to simply accept the fact that someone didn't like me. I thought if someone did not like me I was somehow unlikable. What a trap that was. I spent many years trying to perfect myself to be the best version of me possible. There is nothing wrong with self-actualization. However, my peace should never depend on getting the approval from everyone.

I poured my heart out privately to my Internship supervisor as I told him how unfair it was to be judged not for something I had done, but rather because I reminded my colleague of someone he didn't like, based solely on my external appearance. "Can't he just love me for who I am on the inside?" I asked in tears. "Screw him then. Who needs him." My supervisor issued me a great challenge that changed my life and my ability to truly understand unconditional love. It was a lesson I would never forget. He said, "Tammy you want him to love you unconditionally. But can you do the same? Can you love him even though he rejects you? That is his flaw." The words of my professor were not what I expected to hear. The words humbled me and challenged me to look inside my heart to ask myself if I truly knew how to love unconditionally. It never occurred to me that unconditional love included the ability to love someone who is unable to reciprocate. That was the moment I decided to take the challenge. The pain in my heart melted as I now saw my co-worker as wounded and imperfect. This was my lesson on loving the broken even when they reject me.

Being Beautifully Broken Requires Forgiveness

I cannot finish this chapter without noting that Forgiveness is a necessary component of unconditional love. I cannot love myself unless I forgive myself for my shortcomings. I cannot love others without forgiving them for disappointing me. I cannot live life to the fullest if I hold onto bitterness and unforgiveness. I rob myself basking in the hidden beauty of reconciliation if I shut people out or leave relationships broken.

My father, when employed as a police officer, left my mother for the donut shop lady (no joke). He left us to start a new life. That relationship did not work out. Soon after he moved to the East coast to resume his military career. He later met the perfect woman for him and stayed with her until the end of his life. Most of my life, I talked to my dad on holidays, birthdays, and sometimes in between. For some reason I never resented him for moving on with his life without us. It gave me great joy to see him happy the second half of his life. He must have carried a lot of guilt over his decision though. One of the most touching moments of my life occurred when he was visiting my family for Christmas. He got so much joy spending time with the grandkids. One evening while the children played in the other room Dad took me aside. With tears in his eyes he said, "This is what I missed out on. This is what family is supposed to be like. Will you ever forgive me for leaving?" I melted. Wiping tears from my face

I told him he had been forgiven a long time ago. In that precious moment we held each other as we were both beautifully broken and beautifully reconciled.

Ten years later, I watched my father eat his last meal, a cheeseburger from a local restaurant which he requested us to bring back to him at the hospital. It took him well over an hour and a half to finish his meal. I watched him savor every bite of that cheeseburger. Somehow I knew that would be the last meal he would ever eat. Shortly after he finished I listened to my dad sing the verse to one of his favorite songs, *"Country Road . . . take me home . . . to the place I belong."* My heart was breaking as I heard him sing. The memory of his face in that moment will be with me forever. Family gathered together to honor the memory of his life the next week. His wife, my cousins, and my dear Uncle Lowell ordered his cheeseburger meal in his honor. To honor one man who was beautifully broken but beautifully loved.

I challenge all who read this to look at brokenness in a new way. Don't give up on yourself when life gets you down. Don't shut people out because they are flawed. Strive for reconciliation. Tell people how you feel now. Not just so you can say your peace before you or a loved one nears end of life. Don't miss the opportunity to give and receive the blessing of love, forgiveness, and appreciation . . . so they may have more time to bask in the healing touch of peace that washes over one's soul.

Dedicated to my daughters—Michaela, Jenna and Jessica. May you come to know and always see the beauty that lies within each of you.

I am deeply grateful to those who believed in me when I could not believe in myself. Mom, thank you for never giving up on me! Uncle Lowell, you are my Spiritual mentor and model of unconditional love and are the kindest man I have ever known. I would not be who I am today without your love. Kat, you know me better than anyone and never fail to encourage me even in my darkest hours. Thank you for giving me the opportunity to fulfill a lifelong dream and for pushing me to complete this chapter. I am forever grateful!

~ Tammy Goodspeed

Charlene Carlberg

CHARLENE CARLBERG is an executive coach, author, speaker, and President of Project PAVE.

She resides in Hudson, Florida, with her three beautiful children. Her mission is to break the cycle of all forms of domestic abuse through education. Charlene's project is designed to support any group or individual ready to take the steps to create an extraordinary life. Her poetry is expressions from her heart as she learns and grows in all areas of her life.

charcarlberg@gmail.com
www.charlenecarlberg.com

As the Dominoes Fall

The Unveiling of Self-Love

Lightning punctures the darkness of the small room. Silence, for one … two … and a herd of elephants stampedes across the roof as I gaze at the ceiling. I imagine every drop of rain cleansing me of the pain of dysfunction, the heartache of abuse, the innocence lost. A twin mattress sits on the floor, and I lie atop, staring at my surroundings. To the left, my work clothes neatly hang on a rack borrowed from the high school, where I am the assistant principal, and below, my favorite shoes form a tidy line. The rest of my clothing sits in bags on my left. I've attempted to strategically organize them, a dresser of sacks instead of drawers. I rarely watch anything on the nine-inch television hanging on the wall, but I often turn it on to drown out the noise in my head or the sound of my soon-to-be ex's rantings.

Yes, this ten-by-ten space is where I've slept every night for almost a year now, but not for much longer. The house is over four thousand square feet, but this little room is where I first found a sense of peace. It used to be the weight room. Now it's just my room, or as my children call it, Mom's room. I chose to leave the beautiful master suite because it was littered with the fear and pain of the woman who had been afraid to leave, the woman I was not going to be any longer.

I hadn't had the courage to say no or to stop him when it first started. From the words of humiliation to the frequent rape, I endured the hurt day and night. I didn't feel worthy of anything better than the pain, so I allowed it to continue without comment, without complaint. After all, that was to be expected in a marriage.

My family tree is plagued with alcoholism and abuse. My great-grandmother, grandmother, aunts, mother, all were subservient, codependent on husbands that demonstrated nothing of love or respect, no words of encouragement or care. These were the only relationships I was exposed to. Shame chained my family into a cycle of abuse that seemed unbreakable. The women in my life stayed with their men until the bitter end, till death do them part. Their own mental health and happiness was not relevant. Because nothing could be worse for their children than a broken home. So this was the philosophy I grew up to accept as well. My children deserved a complete family, and if that meant I suffered emotional and sexual abuse, so be it.

For far longer than I'd like to admit, I endured that abusive existence. Until one day I said, "No more!" The journey to "no more" was a bumpy but beautiful road, one that I'd gladly travel again, as it brought me to a new place of peace, of safety. My journey to this twin mattress on the floor of my tiny room began with the discovery of long-forgotten memories, unveiled to me as layers of my past were uncovered. Starting with a rocking chair.

The creaky old rocking chair had been passed down in my family for generations. It was a treasured gift bestowed upon each daughter after the birth of her first child. It was a lucky chair, they said; it brought healing. I had contracted scarlet fever as a baby. I'd been very sick, my mother told me. She'd rocked me in the chair for days, calming me until my fever broke. She smiles every time she tells this story, believing in the miracle of the rocking chair. With each rock she'd visualized me healthy and fever-free, until I was. From the time I was young I'd looked forward to the day that the chair would become mine. It would mean that I'd become a mom. If I had children, I would have value, because I would love them and they would love me.

When I took the pregnancy test at two in the morning, it was unambiguously positive. My heart raced, eyes welled up with tears of incredible joy. I knew my husband would be angry if I woke him at this hour, so I quietly celebrated by myself in the bathroom. I stared at myself in the mirror. I was going to be a mom! It was my greatest dream finally come true.

When I rocked my son in this chair for the first time, I felt a love so strong that I still don't have the words to describe it. I also felt a sudden surge of fear, for him. It awoke in me an intense need to protect him, his safety becoming my complete focus. I hadn't been able to understand it at the time, but I had become determined that my beautiful son would not experience childhood as I had. I wanted to erase my past by protecting his future. There in my arms was the unconditional love I so desperately desired. Rocking him became our special time alone, memories I cherish.

But darkness began to creep into the tender moments. "You're always holding him—put him down!" my husband would complain almost daily. He was jealous of the love and affection I had for our son. He would constantly tell me I was making mistakes in caring for the baby. I didn't understand the change in his personality, but I accepted it. I apologized when he claimed I did something wrong; I smiled and moved on. I couldn't wait to have another child, couldn't wait to fill my heart with more love.

It wasn't long before I was pregnant with baby number two. I felt like the luckiest lady on the planet. I wanted to find out the sex, but my husband said no. Finding that out should be a surprise when the baby was born, and I was selfish for wanting to ruin it for him. I didn't really believe this, but I didn't push back either.

During the pregnancy, I worked part-time as a teacher while caring for my son and my very ill grandmother. She had cardiopulmonary disease and it had advanced to the point where she needed help bathing, dressing, and even eating. She was an amazing spirit, never complaining about her suffering. As I watched her struggle with each breath, I prayed. I prayed that she would live to see my baby born, that she wouldn't leave me too soon. Every afternoon after work I would make her a cup of tea and we would chat while my son played nearby. I felt lucky to have this time with her. After my mother, my grandmother was my biggest cheerleader. She told me I was beautiful and smart. I knew she was wrong about that, but I appreciated the kind words anyway. My husband never missed an opportunity to criticize me about my weight, the way I cleaned the house, the words I used incorrectly. It was exhausting. But I had my son, my mom, my wonderful grandmother, so life was good, I told myself.

As I entered my third trimester, my grandmother was hospitalized. My mom, my sister, and I knew she didn't have much time left, and we were afraid to lose her. I watched her sleeping as if I had to absorb her every feature. She was so thin and frail, yet I saw beauty. Her kindness spread from her core to radiate from her face. I loved her so much. I kissed her gently, and she woke. At her request, I brushed her teeth, and then I sat next to her on her bed. She rubbed my small basketball of a belly and told me I was beautiful, though I felt fat and ugly. When she said she was very tired, I told her to rest, that I'd see her the next day. Unfortunately, there was no next day. She died peacefully in her sleep.

My heart broke. She would never meet my second baby; I'd never again hear her words of encouragement. The night she died, I saw her in a dream. She was healthy and strong. Over and over she said to me, "Char, love and cherish your daughters." *Daughters?* I thought as I woke. Could I be blessed with more than just one?

Three months later I sat in the rocking chair with my precious baby girl. The chair squeaked, and to cover the sound, I sang to her: "You are my sunshine, my only sunshine..." Sunlight indeed surrounded her and she looked angelic as she drifted off to sleep. I closed my own eyes and embraced the love of the newest edition to my family, enjoyed the silence and escape of our time alone together. I dozed off to sleep with visions of my son dancing and singing, "I you, Mommy. I you!" His way of saying he loved me brought a smile to my face.

Suddenly, the scene in my vision took a sinister turn. Playing with my Barbie in the living room, I was an innocent seven-year-old. My babysitter appeared. When I looked at her, I felt a surge of uncertainly. I didn't understand why. Saying nothing, she grabbed my hand and led me to my bedroom. *Why were we going in there?* I was confused. I glanced over at my sister who was engrossed in her TV show. I silently implored her to turn and see me. She didn't notice as I was pulled through the threshold of our bedroom and the door was locked. My heart raced. I wanted to run, but I was frozen in fear. I was panicked, but silent, as she made me sit on the bed. My body shook along with my thoughts. I closed my eyes and escaped to another place in my mind as I waited for it to just be over.

I awoke with a jump to the sound of my daughter's crying. As I looked down at her, tears flooded my eyes and made rivers down my face. The horror of that day, long buried in my memory, had now pushed its way back up to the surface. It invaded my mind, and I tried desperately to push it back under. Shame, so intense that I physically shook, overwhelmed me. I looked down into my daughter's eyes, and then over to my son sleeping on his nearby bed, and vowed to never allow anyone to hurt them. Ever. In that moment I realized why I had felt such a strong urge to protect my children from unidentified harm. The inescapable torture of being molested had been a constant presence in my mind, even while the conscious memory had been suppressed. I was never going to allow this to happen to my children. I wished I had been able to tell my own mother back then what had happened. I wanted to tell someone now. I needed help. And I came to the realization that my upbringing had made my current situation almost inevitable.

Perception was everything, and image was to be protected at all costs. This was the central lesson of my childhood. Living with an alcoholic father taught me to smile through pain. Turn that frown around and pretend life was great, that everything was perfect. The chaos and disorder that ruled the household day and night was never acknowledged. When the smoke cleared, everyone would put on their smile and act like nothing had happened. I developed my own mask, and the art of never letting anyone see the pain I carried inside.

My innocence had been taken away at a very young age, not only by the dysfunction of my family, but by the hands of that trusted teenager. After that night I did what was expected, what I had learned. I woke up the next morning, put a smile on my face, and made sure not a soul would know what had happened to me. My heart couldn't bear the pain or face the reality of what had occurred. To survive, I had to move forward with no visible scars.

I became obsessed with proving to myself and others that my life was perfect. As a young adult I perfected my craft. I was the girl everyone wanted to be around.

Girls were drawn to my warm heart; boys found me physically attractive. I provided a listening ear, sincere advice, and a good laugh when you needed one. My drive to excel socially and academically helped me achieve my goals.

I met my future ex when we were in high school. Though everyone saw me as an open and loving girl, inside I longed for someone to love me unconditionally. I often felt weak and alone; he appeared strong, physically and mentally. Thinking that I'd found my true love, I felt lucky. Desperation to be loved obscured my view of his true nature.

To the outside world, I had the ideal marriage, family, job; behind closed doors my life was a nightmare. I wanted him to stop abusing me; I wanted myself to stop lying about his abuse. I pleaded with him, told him how much he was hurting me. He didn't care. Night after night he expected me to be available for sex. If I fell asleep before he came to bed, I was punished. I almost believed I deserved it. Most nights I would simply lie in bed and wait for his attack. Sometimes I tried to wear pajamas as armor, but it didn't work. "Take that off," he would bark, and my blood would run cold. But in the mornings I would wake to my precious children. My existence revolved around ensuring their health and happiness. There was no cross I wasn't willing to bear for them.

It wasn't until after our third child, a second daughter, was born that I began to face the reality that his behavior was not normal and that I did not deserve it. I became aware of the message I was unintentionally teaching my children, the same lessons I'd learned as a child.

My father's death was the final push I needed. The sights and smells of that day are forever etched in my memory. Only two weeks prior we had been shocked by his diagnosis of advanced lung cancer. As a child, I'd spent countless nights hiding in my room, pressing my legs against the door to prevent him from entering during his alcoholic rages. The metastases in his brain impacted his deep limbic system, which affects mood. In those final weeks, cancer took away his anger just as it would take away his life. He became the father I'd always wished he would be. My mom, my sister, and I took turns wiping the blood from his nose and mouth, watching his skin turn from pale pink to ashy gray. As I watched him cling to life, I recognized for the first time that his own childhood had been just like mine.

A shy boy, he'd ached to prove to the world that he was a strong man. He'd often felt incomplete, not good enough by his family's standards. He'd enlisted in the Navy and was immediately sent to Vietnam. He'd joined to fight for his country, to fight for his manhood. A changed man, he came home to a changed country that was angry at his involvement in the war. Even his father was angry. Having expected to be everyone's hero, he was lost in a sea of disappointment. He turned to alcohol to cope.

His eyes sprung open as he took his last breath. My heart skipped a beat, and I thought I had one more moment with him alive. Then I felt silly. This was no movie; this was real life. My father had passed and there would be no more conversation, no more pain, no more anything. He was gone. It was in that second that I realized the time was now.

I was determined to remove my mask. This meant exposing the façade to my family and the world. It meant facing the fear of the unknown and stopping the cycle of abuse. Most importantly, it meant that I was no longer willing to be the victim of my life. I was ready to start living.

I often pondered what the phrase "start living" meant. How do you begin to define living when you never once allowed yourself to live? I turned to the two pillars of strength in my life: my mom and my sister, for they were the foundation for my courage. I shared what was really happening in my home. Without hesitation they were there for my children and I. Every step I took, they supported. On days when I didn't think I had the energy to go on, they were there to lift me up. When I needed the courage to carry on, they provided it.

~~~

As I drive to work, I see a plane flying high overhead. I watch it until it drifts out of sight. I see myself in that plane, flying, leaving behind the past for a new destination. Geographically, I left the abuse behind about a year after my father passed away. It took longer to move on mentally.

The divorce took its toll on the children and I. Yet, I was grateful for my experiences, for the opportunity to help my children grow through the process, to show them the cycle was breakable after all. There were days when I wanted to hide beneath my cover and not face the world. Times when I felt I didn't have the strength to breathe. Then a random encounter caught me off guard.

It was during the first game of my son's weekend basketball tournament that someone caught my eye.

My son shared my love of watching and playing basketball, and during the first summer after the divorce, I made it a priority to go to all of his tournaments and take him to several NBA games; these were perfect opportunities to get him to open up and talk.

From across the court I watched him coach the opposing team. For the first time since my divorce I was looking at a man, and he sparked a curiosity that I had never felt before. He was handsome, his dark complexion and hair accentuating his athletic body. I studied every detail of how he moved, his expressions as he talked.

After the game, my son and I were discussing the details of his strong performance on the court. I didn't hear him approach, so was startled when I heard him speak. "Excuse me," he said. "Great game. You had a nice shot." Both my son and I beamed with pride. He introduced himself. "It's a pleasure to meet you." He stared directly into my eyes. My heart raced. As I'd watched him earlier, I'd fantasized about going over to talk to him. Now he was standing in front of me and I couldn't seem to do anything but stare. My son noticed my awkwardness and quickly engaged Joel in a discussion of the game. I barely managed a good-bye.

I saw him again during the next day of the tournament. This time I managed to hold a brief conversation with him without my son needing to play wingman. Joel asked for my number, and I gladly provided it.

We texted back and forth over the next few weeks. It was fun and playful, and I was beginning to come to life again. When we first spent the night together, the passion was intense. His soft, gentle touch sent shivers through my body. His tender kiss allowed me to feel the blood flow through my veins. We spent hours pleasuring each other. But I wondered, *Could this be real?*

As he held me in his arms, I melted against him. We talked and shared our life experiences. Joel knew instantly that behind my smile was years of pain. I could feel him embrace my soul. It frightened me. The years of buried emotions prevented me from sharing or even understanding my true feelings. I needed to run. And I did. I left his bed in the middle of the night with the intention of never seeing him again.

Sitting in my car outside his house, a tidal wave of emotions hit me. Thoughts and feelings that I'd never allowed to surface were now flooding my eyes with tears. The pain couldn't be suppressed with a smile or joke. *Why today? Why now?* I asked myself. Raw emotion unleashed like a wild animal flowed through me. I'd spent my life running from the reality of the moment, and now was the time to love myself enough to finally feel the pain inside.

Then he appeared at my window. Through my watery vision, I saw the man who saw through my mask. Joel would not allow me to hide anymore or to run away from us. And neither would I. I'd always believed that men were a source of pain and heartache, but now I'd found a man that touched my soul. I felt a sense of peace and acceptance. I had to go to him, and I did. The time was now!

Finding love was exhilarating. More importantly, through his acceptance, I was able to accept myself for all that I was. My outlook changed, and I embraced a new view.

My dreams were ignited. I began to write, and write, and write. I used writing to heal my mind and address all of my experiences: the good, the bad, the loving, the hurtful, all the joys and pitfalls on the roller coaster of life. I used my poetry to emotionally purge all the past distress and abuse.

As the final layer of my mask peeled away, I discovered that with true unconditional love, everything grows, everything feels possible. The source of that love is found within. At the core of your existence must be self-love. Without it, you are victim to your past, at the mercy of your surroundings, dependent on the acceptance of others.

The time had come for me to release all the demons of my past and grow in the light of love. The truest love, the only love I really ever needed, was deep inside me. And it was a love that abuse could never kill.

Dedicated to Dorothy Rose Kaminskas. Although absent from this earth your voice guides me each day.

To my mom, Donna Carlberg-Eckstein—your unwavering devotion and love is so special to me. You are the strongest most loving woman in the world. I am honored to be your daughter and appreciate all that you have done for our family. I love you more than words could ever say.

~ Charlene Carlberg

Tracey Willms Deane

TRACEY WILLMS DEANE is an artist: sculptor, painter, and author. Currently, Tracey owns and manages a specialist retail store bringing local art and artisan goods to the public. She is an active member in community development groups and leads a Conscious Women's meet up group.

Born and raised in Canada, Tracey has chosen to reside in New Zealand since 1989. She's grateful to have raised two children in this little corner of paradise and finds solace in being in Nature. She loves to sing harmony in an A Capella drop-in choir with a few dozen fellow amateur singers, and to do creative journaling. Together with her husband, Danny, and wee dog, Silky, she enjoys coaxing their clay hill into a cosy home with a small orchard, veggie garden, and paddocks for a few alpacas.

tracey.artinforms@gmail.com
www.tuataradesignstore.com

🐋 Having a Whale of a Time

I have volunteered for this. Left my own "babies" behind for this. Actually, they're "big kids" now — both at school, so I'm bravely letting us each have a growing up step of ten weeks apart. While it rips me up to leave them home, at the same time, the solo space is healing my soul. My paradox of motherhood! But I'm following the trail of opportunities and synchronicities that opened up through conversations with a friend, whose friend had a friend … allowing me to fulfil a lifetime dream. I can at least soothe myself with the knowing that I'm showing my kids a good role model of following your dreams.

I'm not exactly a morning person, but here I am in the Kingdom of Tonga, gladly getting up at sunrise, six days a week. It's the middle of August, which is wintertime in the southern hemisphere. Here in the tropics, it is warm during the days, but cooling somewhat overnight, especially if it rains. I wake up as I stand under the cold shower (there's no hot water in my Fale) and briskly rub dry with my towel. Breakfast is some local mango, papaya and imported cornflakes with juice (no milk will keep without a refrigerator). Wearing the daily uniform of swimsuit, shorts, t-shirt, sunhat, sunglasses and flip-flops, takes me back to my teen years working as a lifeguard. I'm not quite as slim and fit as I was then, but older and wiser now, more experienced with people and the world, and still strong enough to do this job. Glad of the lack of mirrors to show me my midriff rolls, I happily stuff another towel, my camera, and my raincoat in a bag over my shoulder and I'm off down the sandy path to the resort's dive centre. Amongst the jungle of dive tanks and breathing gear, I have to sort through the available sizes of wetsuits, fins, masks and snorkels to kit out today's boatload of whale-watchers. The dive instructors are kitting out their clients too, preparing to go out on a different boat than us. It's calmly chaotic in the cramped concrete equipment room. By 08:30h we've got four bins full of gear, the lunch, and the captain's camera gear—including underwater housings—"Be careful with that!!"—all piled onto the hand-pulled trolley ready to wheel it down to the beach.

Rattling past Fales 10 through 14 of the resort, trying to not talk too loudly and wake up any late-sleeping guests, we pad single file like a string of baby ducks after their mother. Two or three guides, depending on guest numbers, which can be 16 maximum, plus the captain/owner of the boat. Rounding the corner, we reach the end of the concrete path and ditch our sandals under the tree. The rest of the day will be barefoot. The trolley's wheels will not turn through the deep sand of the beach, so it's parked to the side and its time to start carrying all the bins of gear to the water's edge. Whoever drew the short straw that day gets to be the Roper. One of the crew is on board setting up. One is on the beach getting guests ready and helping them into the dingy. The inflatable dingy can hold six to eight adults, so that's three trips most days. The Roper ferries the passengers, crew and gear from beach to boat by pulling the dingy along the two-inch thick rope that goes between the shoreline and our forty-foot (twelve metre) catamaran—a trip of about fifty metres, depending on the tide. It's eco-friendly: no fuel pollution and no machinery breakdowns to deal with in this remote island setting. The rope is waterlogged though so it sinks. It's also a popular home for algae growth, making it slippery. Best not to drop it once you get going! The workout is great for toning arms, legs, back and abs, and you soon get a reading on the personalities you have with you today. So the Roper position has a lot going for it—if you're up for it.

By 9am we are all on board, ready to be briefed on the protocols and safety measures mandatory for our day ahead. The guides are each assigned three or four people to be our group for the day. We talk them through what they can expect, and what not to expect, getting to swim with a whale is not guaranteed! This is a privilege that the whales grant to us, on their terms, and we have no power over it. Nature is not at our beck and call! We prepare the guests as much as possible to get the most out of the window of opportunity that might, hopefully, be presented to us. The conditions of the water and weather, the mood and activities of the whales we encounter, and the swimming ability of the guests all factor into whether we can actually get in the water for an interaction. Or whether we'll just be grateful for all the encounters we can witness from the boat that day—which are pretty special in their own right, and plentiful at this time of year. It reminds me of the Serenity Prayer:

God, grant me the serenity to accept the things
I cannot change,
Courage to change the things I can,
And wisdom to know the difference.

~ REINHOLD NIEBUHR

Basically, unless the whales are at rest, or in a playful "hanging around" curious mood, we can't get in the water with them because by the time we slow the boat down they'll already be gone. Their grace is deceptive, they look to be slow moving but their speed and agility is incredible!

On a good day though, we'll find a "mom and toddler" who are willing to receive visitors while they are resting. You can tell by how the momma reacts to the boat stopping 100m away and just observing for a few minutes. If she dives and resurfaces a short distance away, we will move along too, but only two more times. After that it would be harassment. If she's willing though, she'll stay pretty stationary and we scramble to get our gear on and slip quietly into the water one group at a time. Only a few minutes before the next group's turn, so every second is precious and we swim as fast as we can without making splashes. After all the adrenaline of getting within range, it can be quite a stunning moment to suddenly realize "there she is!" In the vastness of the ocean, by her free will, she is allowing us to visit. We come to a floating stop ten or twelve meters away and just wait, observe, and swim to keep up if there is a current so we don't get drifted away. Sometimes, if Junior is a curious kid, he'll pop out from behind mom to have a look at us. Surfacing to breathe four times more often than his mother means that he is moving around a lot more than her. She is conserving her energy to be able to produce the hundred litres of milk per day that sees her baby gain forty-five kilograms per day, without eating anything herself during this time. In her three months postpartum she'll likely have suitors and will either fend them off or participate in courting chases and mating. And then, by October, she still needs to have enough energy to swim four or five thousand kilometres back to the summer feeding ground! Here's an example of aeons of wisdom, literally thirty million years, of refining how to live well on this planet Earth. Wisdom carried from generation to generation setting up a sustainable, civilized, peaceful, and enjoyable culture.

It's been a few minutes of waiting and watching the baby come closer to us on each circuit, swimming past us to the surface for a breath then back down to cuddle under mum's chin, or her tail, or between her pectoral fins. They are the longest "arms" — proportionately — of any mammal: four to five metres long, one third of her body length. I marvel at how much the baby stays in physical contact with his momma, just like any baby wants and needs skin time. Then I wonder why I was surprised. Perhaps because these are water beings instead of land beings and for the past few centuries, western culture has considered human intelligence to be the only valid kind on earth. Even though consciously I would disagree with that, my surprise showed me an unconscious belief that I was being led by. Glad to see it so I could weed it out. Watching momma give baby a hug with those extra-long fins…so sweet!

We will have to return to the boat soon, but momma seems calm and accepting of our presence so I signal my group to stay close to me and we go up just a little closer toward her head, but not nearer than eight meters so she has plenty of room to move. We stay in her line of sight at all times. It is a safety courtesy for her and for us and allows trust to form. We are not surrounding her so she's not threatened, and while she can see us, she also won't be accidently wiping us out with a flick of her five-metre-wide tail. Now comes the moment of awe. We are floating on the surface of the Pacific Ocean, insignificant as little corks. We're within clear visibility of this creature the size of a bus, whose very large EYE is following our every move and whose very palpable heart PRESENCE can be felt physically inside our own chests. I gaze in gratitude, wondering what her heart feels about us? I send her thanks in my mind and my heart for allowing us to visit, to meet her and her new precious child so close-up in their own home.

By now it's been several minutes since we left the boat, which is holding its position down current from us. It's time for momma to breathe, and with minimal adjustments to her flukes and tail, she rises to exhale, showering us in her spray. She immediately deeply inhales and with a curvature of her spine glides below again. Junior has bobbed up to the surface too and is struggling a bit with his ballast adjustment. But he manages to grab a breath and swims beside momma the whole way as they sink into their next resting place and we reluctantly bid them farewell. We turn and start the swim back to the boat, crossing paths with the next group at the halfway point. There are a few excited squeals in the snorkels, then we remember to keep quiet and calm — we're in the nursery after all. Junior may be three to four metres long (nine to twelve feet long), but he is only a wobbly toddler still.

The next day begins the same way and the weather has that blessed stillness that creates picture-perfect scenes. Although, we'll need to motor longer if there's no wind for sailing, so it seems there's always a pro and a con in any situation. After a morning of only a few distant sightings, there is a palpable feeling of disappointment forming on deck. Then whoosh! Look to starboard—a breach! Not far away—and another breach, close together! We have two adolescent whales frolicking just five hundred metres away. Instantly the despondency evaporates. We are excited, straining with anticipation to see where they will come up next. Again and again the whales are soaring out of the water to well past their midlines, twisting and arching, then falling back to the surface with resounding splashes—clearly having fun and not going anywhere. Our captain cuts our engine and just lets the momentum bring us a bit closer to the whales without rushing in. This is their home so we use our manners: always knock and wait. In this instance, there is no question that they are in the mood for play. One whale surfaces right next to our hull and turns on his side, his three-meter pectoral fin waving lazily in the air at us. "Nice to see you," says his companion, with a spy hop on the other side of the boat. It is action-stations on deck now, let me tell you! Everyone scrambling into their gear at once. Only one group in the water with the whales at a time, but the next group can be right on the edge of the access platform, ready to change over. These two young whales are as curious about us as we are about them. Rolling over on their sides to look up at us, or even on their back so we can observe the deeply grooved throat that extends halfway to their navel. Ever so gently, always keeping us at safe distance they swim around, under, and beside us. At times following each other, other times separated out a bit, but always coming back to us again and again, eye to eye with every group more than once! Such a rare and exquisite treat... I felt like time stood still, then went too fast.

Eventually we got hungry and worn out (none of us is an Olympic swimmer!) and the whales started to head away. But they remained nearby, playing and breaching. I didn't want to get out of the water, didn't want our interaction to end. But we are only human, and sometimes "needs must." When we hove-to in the lee of a small islet for lunchtime, we could still see them surfacing less than a kilometre away.

Much excited chatter amongst us all carried on through lunchtime. Those who, being less water confident, had chosen to enjoy the spectacle from the safety of the deck shared with us their perspective too. This provided much valuable context, enriching our understanding of what we had each experienced. We're always in the right place at the right time for our next lesson. Every heart was flung wide open. From the fearful cautionary mum to the left-brain dominant banker. From the exuberant farmer, to the shy teenager. All so moved. Joyous. Calm. Peaceful. Happy. Here, I thought to myself, is a demonstration from the ultimate wisdom keepers. These whales live and travel in family groups, they do not wage war on each other, they work collectively to gather food during the feeding season, and travel to the tropics for the winter every year. When they're not being hunted by humans, or having their home poisoned with pollution, they live a lifestyle most people would aspire to. Naturally. Our hearts were overflowing. One woman I remember was quite speechless for some time! We made sure she was all right, then we just allowed her space to integrate her experience.

Wisdom from the wild heart speaks to me when I ask, "What would the most highly evolved version of Me be and do naturally?" This is what I aspire to: bringing awareness to unconscious behaviours, strengthening some habits and losing others. By being aware of the synchronicities in my days, and acting on the intuitions that come in, my life becomes more fulfilling, peaceful and enjoyable.

I appreciate the loving support of my family and friends, always. I am in awe at the wisdom and beauty of Nature in all ways. I feel giant gratitude to all the lovely whales and dolphins I have been privileged to swim with, they welcomed me into their world and showed me so much.

Dedicated to the next generation of Wild Hearts, with all my love!

~ Tracey Willms Deane

Sumya Anani

SUMYA ANANI is founder of Learning2Fly, an aerial fitness and wellness center in Kansas City. She is a registered yoga teacher, fitness instructor, former 4x world champion boxer. Her fights have been carried on international TV including ESPN and the undercard of HBO. She speaks publicly, sharing her 'Eye of the Tiger' mindset with individuals, corporations, women's groups, and other organizations.

Teaching yoga is Sumya's passion. Bring your curiosity, playfulness, and fasten your seatbelt for fun and awakening. She guides people in lively, transformational weekend workshops through the seven chakras combining yoga for all abilities, art, writing, discussion, bioenergetic work, and the Heal Your Life program. Workshops vary according to the group's focus.

In 2017, she's launching an online fitness and nutrition program with her son Matthew, who is a yoga teacher and health educator. Contact her if you're interested in bringing her to your studio, group, or gathering.

Newsletter sign up at www.Sumya.com
www.iAMLearning2Fly.com
Sumya@iAMLearning2Fly.com

❧ In Search of Buried Treasure

I have always been drawn to stories of explorers crossing unchartered oceans, or traversing wild forests on a grand adventure. The Lewis and Clark expedition of the uncharted west, Ponce de Leon's search for the Fountain of Youth, and Francisco Coronado's search for the seven fabled cities of gold left me in awe. I wanted to be an explorer too. These treasure hunters, and others like them, were in search of new lands and fortunes of every kind.

When I was a little girl, I loved exploring the woods surrounding the apartments I lived in, pretending to be an explorer. Though adventurous as a young girl, I was also insecure. But when I found myself with a baby at the age of eighteen, I knew I had to grow up fast. I spent four years at a junior college getting my associates degree, then two years in massage school. When presented with an opportunity to live in Jamaica, I couldn't say no. My adventurous spirit kicked in.

Jamaica was a chance to be an explorer, to have my own Sumya Anani expedition. So off I went — from living with my mom to living in a third world country with my young son, Matthew. I taught yoga and gave massages at the Negril Yoga Centre. Matthew and I spent a lot of time together. We have always been very close. It was an amazing time of spiritual growth.

My friend and future boxing trainer, Barry Becker, welcomed me home two years later. I agreed to my first professional boxing match with only three weeks to train. He said I could be a world champion. My internal dialogue didn't agree.

Me ... a world champion ... But I have never watched a boxing match ... I never played sports in high school ... I'm not an athlete ... no way.

Barry had been trying to get me to box for years — with no luck. My world was focused on healing, being a mom, teaching yoga, giving massages. Boxing didn't fit in with these healing arts, or so I thought.

In spite of my fears and doubts, three weeks later I stepped through the ropes into the 'squared circle' for an adventure of another kind — my first professional boxing match. The 'Island Girl' was born. That was my new ring moniker since I had just returned from the Caribbean. Little did I know that boxing and yoga would be crucial foundations for the construction of my self-esteem. Little did I dream that I would use these skills in my work with countless other women that would eventually cross my path.

Our Journey Through the Chakras

As a yoga teacher, I love everything about yoga, even the Sanskrit language. 'Siddhi' is a Sanskrit word pronounced like city, and it means power. We all have seven chakras, or energy centers—our seven powers.

Coronado never found the legendary seven cities of gold. But it has occurred to me that maybe the legend was really referring to the seven siddhi's of gold. Perhaps Coronado's outer quest for treasure was really meant to be an inner quest.

Throughout human history, we have explored the depths of the oceans, the heights of the mountains, and the infinity of outer space. But our capacities within are still remotely understood. In this Aquarian age, many are awakening and realizing the most valuable treasures that are latent inside us.

Every explorer needs a map. We have one for this internal expedition. It is our chakra system—our internal map, constantly guiding us to our highest good. By following the terrain, we can discover and harness seven internal cities of gold. I love guiding women and men, yogis and non-yogis, through personal adventures of the seven chakras. Let's begin this inner journey and discover these golden treasures that lie within.

What is your dream, dear explorer? Lewis and Clark discovered the treasure of the western North American continent. What treasures are within you ready to be discovered? What powers lie within you to create an empowered life, and help to build healthy communities and a better world?

 When you are inspired by some great purpose, some extraordinary project, all your thoughts break their bonds; your mind transcends limitations, your consciousness expands in every direction, and you find yourself in a new, great and wonderful world. Dormant forces, faculties and talents become alive, and you discover yourself to be a greater person by far than you ever dreamed yourself to be.

~ PATANJALI

Let's take the first step on this spiritual expedition in search of your seven siddhis of gold.

Chakra Seven — Thoughts

Thoughts are the building blocks of our lives. Yoga is the art of deliberate creation, and creation begins with a thought. To consciously create, be on the lookout for thoughts that are not in alignment with what you want in your life. This awareness is the first step on your quest.

 We are what we think. All that we are arises with our thoughts. With our thoughts we make the world.

~ THE DHAMMAPADA

I am so grateful I started yoga and meditation before I started boxing. Preparing for a boxing match requires intense physical workouts—weight training, hitting the heavy bags, sparring, swimming, yoga, and more. These workouts lasted 4-6 hours a day. I also had to put my mind through rigorous training with positive affirmations that were foreign at first.

I believe in myself. I can do anything I set my mind to. I am strong.

Stepping in the boxing ring was the scariest thing I've ever done. I came face to face with my worst opponent: my negative, limiting, self-defeating inner dialogue. Becoming aware of my thought patterns was an awakening. I realized that positive thinking had to be the first step towards creating positive changes in my life. To become champion of the world, I realized I had to become champion of my inner world first. I had to master my thoughts.

As a personal trainer, when I help a woman reshape her body I am also helping her reshape the thoughts she has about herself. I have been coaching women to love themselves long before the term "life coach" came into vogue. I took some formal training with Louise Hay's program, becoming a Heal Your Life, life coach. I love sharing methods of self-transformation that have been valuable in my own life. Loving ourselves is an important aspect of health, and helping others learn to love themselves has become a central theme in my 'Sumya Anani expedition.'

And you, dear wanderer, what do you want to believe about yourself? What do you want to become true for you?

I can do anything I set my mind to. I love myself exactly as I am. I direct my thoughts in life-affirming ways.

Chakra Six — Insight

The thoughts we think become images in our mind. Creating an inner vision of who you want to be or what you want to manifest is the next step on your journey. The inner precedes the outer. We are always creating images in our mind. With every vision, we increase the capacity to make our dreams come true. This principle holds true: as above — in the mind, so below — in the body.

 Your imagination is your preview of
life's coming attractions.

~ ALBERT EINSTEIN

As a boxer, I had to picture the end in mind. I practiced visualizing my performance in the ring. To be-come a champion, I had to create the image of a champion.

Footwork didn't come naturally to me in the boxing ring. I never played soccer, basketball, or other running sports. I felt a little awkward on my flat feet, and wasn't a natural at moving around the ring. I was strong standing in one place, but my opponents weren't going to stand still. I practiced visualization, seeing myself moving on my feet with grace and ease. This helped create the outer effect, and my footwork improved with practice. My favorite line from The Million Dollar Baby: "It's the magic of risking everything for a dream that nobody sees but you."

 I have learned that if one advances confidently
in the direction of his dreams, and endeavors to
live the life he has imagined, he will meet with
a success unexpected in common hours.

~ HENRY DAVID THOREAU

Dear visionary, what dreams do you harbor that, as of now, no one else can see but you? The sixth chakra is your inner vision board. Practice seeing what you want on the inner planes first. Then, you can truly accomplish anything you set your mind to.
My visions are powerful forces for good. I see goodness and abundance wherever I turn.

Chakra Five — Communication

With positive thoughts and internal images to match, we discover the treasure of the fifth chakra: the power of our words. To put it simply, words have power.

 Words can inspire. And words can destroy. Choose yours well.

~ ROBIN SHARMA

At Learning2Fly, my aerial fitness, health, and wellness studio in Kansas City, I sometimes hear people say in their first class:

I'm not strong. I can't do this. My upper body is weak. I'll never be good at this.

So I came up with a few rules.

Rule number one: You can only use the word "can't" in this sentence — "There's nothing I can't do."

Rule number two: Only speak positively about yourself.

When a rule is broken, we lovingly reward the 'winner' with ten pushups followed by the requirement to rephrase the statement in a positive way.

In boxing, this is called counter punching. The opponent throws a punch. I bob and weave my head, slip the punch, and throw my own punch back. So at Learning2Fly, we counterpunch every negative comment with a positive one.

"My upper body is so weak" becomes *"I'm getting stronger every day."*

"I can't do that" becomes *"I am unable to do that at this moment."*

When a 'c' word is spoken, the offender also puts a quarter in the 'Quarters for Can't' donation jar. It truly is a reward because they're getting stronger with every pushup they do. The money goes to a local charity at the end of the year. It feels good to recycle our negatives and do something positive in our communities. Students love this little ritual as it brings many laughs, but also an awareness of negative internal dialogues and self-talk.

 Use the power of your word in the direction of truth and love.

~ DON MIGUEL RUIZ

Saying we can't do something is a lie we tell ourselves. Who says we're supposed to be good at something the first time we try? With this requirement, we wouldn't have art, the Statue of Liberty, airplanes, the Olympics, or computers.

Nothing would have been accomplished in the world if we had to get it right the first time.

Remember, what we say about ourselves may become true for us. So it's important to be aware of our words and replace them with what we actually want to create. It's the law of substitution at work.

Dear traveler, can you start speaking to yourself like you would to a loved one? *Good morning precious. You're amazing. Keep up the good work. I love you.*

Chakra Four — Love

We have seen the remarkable potential of the mind when it comes to technology. Humans have invented electricity, air conditioning, cellphones, and spaceships to fly to the moon — to name a few. Now it's time to unlock the potential of the heart.

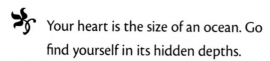 Your heart is the size of an ocean. Go
find yourself in its hidden depths.

~ RUMI

The heart chakra calls you to gather your allies and form your dream team. Love comes in the form of wisdom and support from the people who will be part of your journey.

Recognizing the need for help and asking for it is difficult for some people, but we need others to help us fulfill our greatness. The U.S. government helped Lewis and Clark embark on their exploration of the west. Along the way, Native American Indians guided them to explore their territories. Friends and allies, new and old, support us in many ways — teaching us new skills, helping us through challenges, listening to us vent, and in general, being our cheerleader. Rah! Rah!

As a writer, I rely on my editor to help me use words with clarity. As a business owner, I rely on my business advisor who has years of experience working with small and large businesses. When I was boxing, I needed my trainer, Barry Becker, to teach me the art of protecting myself.

With my boxing trainer's love, encouragement, guidance, and affirmation, I won four world championships in three weight classes. I was voted *Most Avoided Female Fighter in the World* two years in a row. My thoughts, visions, and words were fundamental to success, but Barry was the glue behind the power of 'The Island Girl.' I wouldn't have accomplished what I did without him.

Learning is a lifelong process, starting as children. Good parents understand the importance of love, positive reinforcement, and encouragement. In Jamaica, Matthew and I would sit journaling for hours by the beach. He would draw with crayons. I ooohed and awwwed over each page he created and hung it proudly on the wall. I told him what an amazing artist he was. I bragged to my friends and showed them his art. As adults, we still need this positive affirmation. We never outgrow this.

Love can sometimes turn to misunderstanding and hurt. We need to release any resentment arising from this, in particular any negative thoughts we might be harboring towards our parents, caregivers, or anyone along the way who has come up short or 'done us wrong.' Bitterness and anger block the power of the heart chakra. We must accept that our parents truly did the best they could and would have done better if they knew how.

Louise Hay helped me learn this lesson. Her story is beautifully told through her book and movie; *You Can Heal Your Life.* Her life journey has been a testimony to the power of love, forgiveness, and acceptance—primary tasks of the heart chakra.

 Forgiving yourself and others will release
you from the prison of the past.

~ LOUISE HAY

Look around, dear wanderer, and thank your cheerleaders who love and support you. See how the love and skills of other people help move you towards your dreams.

Everyone is a golden link in the chain of my highest good.

Another aspect of the heart chakra is to meditate on how your dreams will benefit others. My athletic dreams have allowed me to teach countless women self-defense. My love of yoga has guided me to promote peacefulness and acceptance in the world. As a writer, I hope to inspire readers to make healthy changes in their lives.

Dear voyager, the world needs you. How will your realized dreams contribute to the healing of people and planet? Meditate on this. Your unique gifts make a difference for us all.

My life is a blessing to my family, my community, and to the world.

Chakra Three — Purposeful Action

 Efforts and courage are not enough
without purpose and direction.

~ JOHN F. KENNEDY

I love the word 'potential.' It has several meanings in the dictionary.

1. Capable of being, but not yet in existence.
2. Having possibility, capability, or power.
3. Something possessing the capacity for growth or development.
4. The act or instance of transforming.

The third chakra is fire, and fire is the ultimate transformer. It takes perseverance and discipline to do work. Action is required to make things happen in the world, and to unearth our dormant treasures. In order to realize my potential as a boxer, it wasn't enough to affirm and visualize myself as a champion.

Dreams get you started; discipline keeps you going.

~ JIM ROHN

I had to discipline myself. A daily, rigorous training schedule was required. Close attention to my food choices was critical. Meditation helped undo negative patterns of thinking, replacing them with positive thoughts. Rest and sleep were real priorities, so I had to limit activities with friends. Many sacrifices were made to realize my dream of becoming a world champion.

Dear pilgrim, what practices do you need to include or eliminate from your life in order to achieve your dream? Are you willing to make the sacrifices necessary and do the work required? Can you set healthy boundaries, saying "yes" when you need to say yes and "no" when you must say no? With persistence, determination, and clarity you can take inventory on a daily basis in making those decisions. Every action you take guides you to your destiny.

I harness my power to explore my unique gifts and talents. I make choices that serve me in positive ways. I set healthy boundaries that are in alignment with my dreams.

Chakra Two — Passion

Learning to adapt and go with the flow is essential as we move through life since change is the only constant. Flowing through transitions with grace and ease, and following our passions is fundamental in navigating the waters of change represented by the second chakra.

 Tell me, what is it you plan to do with your
one wild and precious life?

~ MARY OLIVER

Health, fitness, and wellness are my passions. I have always wanted a healing center, yoga studio, or gym of some kind. I knew it would never happen when I was boxing because the training schedule was too demanding. As I was in transition from being a professional fighter to _____?_____, I wandered into an aerial fitness class in Colorado looking for another physical avenue after boxing.

I started forming and shaping my own health curriculum for kids by teaching kid's summer camps at a community college. This program is now called 'A Chakra Circus of Health.' We teach kids seven habits of health in creative and engaging ways. My vision: These seven habits of health will positively revolutionize the world!

I also followed my passion for health by taking journalism classes at the community college. I want to develop a health program on TV for families. We need more positive programming on television.

Change requires trust, going with the flow of your passions, and sometimes sitting with uncertainty. Major changes in life aren't usually easy. But staying true to self is essential to transition.

For any transitions you might be experiencing, dear reader, take time to sit and ask yourself, 'What am I passionate about?'

I flow through change with grace and ease. My passions are always guiding me towards my highest good.

Chakra One — And So It Is

The first chakra is seeing your goal come to fruition. This completes the cycle that began with just a thought.

Two years after my first professional boxing match, I defeated the only female boxer to appear on the cover of Sports Illustrated. Five years later, I won my first world championship. The following year, I earned three more. By following the map of the chakras, my thoughts had been brought to fruition. I continue to use the inner compass of the chakras in my own life to create success, joy, and abundance.

I love threading the ancient wisdom of yoga and the chakras with powerful personal development techniques in transformative weekend workshops. These seven treasures are within you, guiding you to your highest good. Your talents and gifts are contributions that are meant to benefit the world.

 You are here to enable the world to live more amply, with greater vision, and with a finer spirit of hope and achievement. You are here to enrich the world, and you impoverish yourself if you forget this errand.

~ WOODROW WILSON

I love helping people implement my seven healthy habits for mind, body, and spirit. I love guiding students at Learning2Fly and in classes and workshops at yoga studios, community centers, in women's groups, and in the corporate world. My profession, passion, and purpose is to help others navigate their way to personal empowerment and happiness.

Everyone benefits from this work. Yoga is not just for the fit, thin, flexible or athletic. The journey is for everyone. It's time we discover the treasures within to realize and fulfill our potential. When used wisely, your seven siddhi's of gold are a blessing to the world. You must go in search and discover them for yourself. They are only to be found by searching within. Your adventure is waiting.

 Life is either a daring adventure or nothing.

~ HELEN KELLER

Dear fellow adventurer, I don't know where the 'Sumya Anani expedition' will take me from here, but I do hope to meet you along the way. I pray your '_____' expedition is blessed with love, light, joy, passion, and peace. Amen.

To the creative Spirit, and to its expression.

To the genius each of us own.

To the adventure that is our life.

To the discovery of our unique potentials.

May my life be a gift to the world.

Thank you Spirit, for the visions that dance in my head.

Amen

To my parents for the gift of life.

To Matthew, my son and gift of God.

To Barry, my boxing trainer, friend, boyfriend—you have
changed my whole life for the better. To my friends who
have supported me.

To everyone who has ever been part of my story. You made a
difference.

I am grateful for everyone undergoing their own spiritual
adventure of awakening. Together, we will rock this world
with love and joy. You are all making a difference, and I
bow in humble gratitude for your courage and commitment
to living authentically.

Thank you for E=mc2.

~Sumya Anani

Today Is A NEW Day

Today is a NEW day,
    And I have something to say.
I'm here with a lot to release, you see,
    I'm letting it go for the sake of me.
I can't keep it inside; I have to let it go,
    It's time for me to reach inside and grow.
I want a new life, not just be,
    I want to be happy, I want to be free!!
I want it all to go away,
    I want only the positive to stay.
I'm letting this go, which is a wonderful start,
    I'm releasing it ALL from my heart.
I've searched my heart and rattled my brain,
    By doing this, I know it'll keep me sane.
I'm facing my demons and searching my soul,
    I'm gonna do my best to get out of this hole.
I won't go back to the place I was before,
    I want to be happy and let my spirit soar.
I have the confidence, I will not fail,
    Just waiting for the wind to catch my sail.
I have letters that I could never send,
    I release them to the heavens and the wind.
I also have the ugly thoughts of myself that roll around in my head,
    They will no longer hold me and wish I was dead.
To let this go will bring me peace,
    And the pain will finally cease.
I'm here and sharing this with you,
    Here's to being honest with ourselves and true!
Today is a new day,
    Releasing my negatives is the only way.

–Sue Young

Reference/Bibliography

A Course in Miracles, Foundation for Inner Peace

Angelou, Maya, *Peaceful Quotes*; Peaceatseven.com

Buddha, Gautama. <u>The Dhammapada</u>. Collection of Sayings of the Buddha.

Dyer, W. Dr.: Facebook: 28 August 2015

Dyer Family: Facebook: 31 August 2015

Harrell, Keith D. (2004) *Everyday Positive Thinking—Attitude is Everything Cards* by Keith D. Harrell, Hay House, Inc.

Hay, Louise, *Louise Hay Quotes and Sayings*; inspiringquotesus.com

Hay, Louise. <u>You Can Heal Your Life</u>. Carlsbad: Hay House, January 1, 1984.

Holmes, Ernest, *The Science of Mind* (1926) revised edition by Ernest Holmes and Maude Allison Latham (1938) Tarcher Putnam

Kennedy, John F. Senator Kennedy's Speech. Coliseum. Raleigh: September 17, 1960.

Myss, Caroline and Occhiogrosso, Peter (2004) *Everyday Positive Thinking—Healing Cards* by Caroline Myss and Peter Occhiogrosso, Hay House, Inc.

Nepo, Mark (2000) *The Book of Awakinging—Having the Life You Want by Being Present to the Life You Have*, Conari Press

Ruiz, Don Miguel. The Four Agreements: A Practical Guide to Personal Freedom. San Rafael: Amber-Allen Publishing, November 1997.

Oliver, Mary. "The Summer Day." House of Light. Boston: Beacon Press, 1990.

Sharma, Robin. The 50 New Rules of Work. Online blog.

Song: Already Gone; Artists: *The Eagles Album: On the Border* 1974; Written By: Jack Tempchin and Robb Strandlund

Song: All You Need is Love; Artists: *The Beatles Album: Magical Mystery Tour* 1967; Written By: John Lennon and Paul McCartney

The Top Five Regrets of the Dying: A life transformed by the dearly departed., Hayhouse, Inc.

Thoreau, Henry. Walden. Boston: Ticknor and Fields, August 9, 1854.

Ware, Bronnie (2011)

Wilson, Woodrow. "Address of President Wilson." Swarthmore College, Swarthmore. October 25, 1913.

Resources

The following list of resources are for the national headquarters; search in your yellow pages under "Community Services" for your local resource agencies and support groups.

AIDS
CDC National AIDS Hotline
(800) 342-2437

ALCOHOL ABUSE

Al-Anon Family Group Headquarters
1600 Corporate Landing Parkway
Virginia Beach, VA 23454-5617
(888) 4AL-ANON
www.al-anon.alateen.org

Alcoholics Anonymous (AA)
General Service Office
475 Riverside Dr., 11th Floor
New York, NY 10115
(212) 870-3400
www.alcoholics-anonymous.org

Children of Alcoholics Foundation
164 W. 74th Street
New York, NY 10023
(800) 359-COAF
www.coaf.org

Mothers Against Drunk Driving
MADD
P.O. Box 541688
Dallas, TX 75354
(800) GET-MADD
www.madd.org

National Association of Children of Alcoholics (NACoA)
11426 Rockville Pike, #100
Rockville, MD 20852
(888) 554-2627
www.nacoa.net

Women for Sobriety
P.O. Box 618
Quartertown, PA 18951
(215) 536-8026
www.womenforsobriety.org

CHILDREN'S RESOURCES

Child Molestation

ChildHelp USA/Child Abuse Hotline
15757 N. 78th St.
Scottsdale, AZ 85260
(800) 422-4453
www.childhelpusa.org

Prevent Child Abuse America
200 South Michigan Avenue, 17th Floor
Chicago, IL 60604
(312) 663-3520
www.preventchildabuse.org

Crisis Intervention

Girls and Boys Town National Hotline
(800) 448-3000
www.boystown.org

Children's Advocacy Center of East Central Illinois
(If your heart feels directed to make a donation to this center,
please include Lisa Hardwick's name in the memo)
616 6th Street
Charleston, IL 61920
(217) 345-8250
http://caceci.org

Children of the Night
14530 Sylvan St.
Van Nuys, CA 91411
(800) 551-1300
www.childrenofthenight.org

National Children's Advocacy Center
210 Pratt Avenue
Huntsville, AL 35801
(256) 533-KIDS (5437)
www.nationalcac.org

Co-Dependency

Co-Dependents Anonymous
P.O. Box 33577
Phoenix, AZ 85067
(602) 277-7991
www.codependents.org

Suicide, Death, Grief

AARP Grief and Loss Programs
(800) 424-3410
www.aarp.org/griefandloss

Grief Recovery Institute
P.O. Box 6061-382
Sherman Oaks, CA 91413
(818) 907-9600
www.grief-recovery.com

Suicide Awareness Voices of Education
Minneapolis, MN 55424
(952) 946-7998
Suicide National Hotline
(800) 784-2433

DOMESTIC VIOLENCE

National Coalition Against Domestic Violence
P.O. Box 18749
Denver, CO 80218
(303) 831-9251
www.ncadv.org

National Domestic Violence Hotline
P.O. Box 161810
Austin, TX 78716
(800) 799-SAFE
www.ndvh.org

DRUG ABUSE

Cocaine Anonymous National Referral Line
(800) 347-8998
National Helpline of Phoenix House
(800) COCAINE
www.drughelp.org

National Institute of Drug Abuse
(NIDA)
6001 Executive Blvd., Room 5213,
Bethesda, MD 20892-9561, Parklawn
Building
Info: (301) 443-6245
Help: (800) 662-4357
www.nida.nih.gov

EATING DISORDERS

Overeaters Anonymous
National Office
P.O. Box 44020
Rio Rancho, NM 87174-4020
(505) 891-2664
www.overeatersanonymous.org

GAMBLING

Gamblers Anonymous
International Service Office
P.O. Box 17173
Los Angeles, CA 90017
(213) 386-8789
www.gamblersanonymous.org

HEALTH ISSUES

American Chronic Pain Association
P.O. Box 850
Rocklin, CA 95677
(916) 632-0922
www.theacpa.org

American Holistic Health Association
P.O. Box 17400
Anaheim, CA 92817
(714) 779-6152
www.ahha.org

The Chopra Center at La Costa Resort and Spa Deepak Chopra, M.D.
2013 Costa Del Mar
Carlsbad, CA 92009
(760) 494-1600
www.chopra.com

The Mind-Body Medical Institute
110 Francis St., Ste. 1A
Boston, MA 02215
(617) 632-9530 Ext. 1
www.mbmi.org

National Health Information Center
P.O. Box 1133
Washington, DC 20013-1133
(800) 336-4797
www.health.gov/NHIC

Preventive Medicine Research Institute
Dean Ornish, M.D.
900 Brideway, Ste 2
Sausalito, CA 94965
(415) 332-2525
www.pmri.org

MENTAL HEALTH

American Psychiatric Association of America
1400 K St. NW
Washington, DC 20005
(888) 357-7924
www.psych.org

Anxiety Disorders Association of America
11900 Parklawn Dr., Ste. 100
Rockville, MD 20852
(310) 231-9350
www.adaa.org

The Help Center of the American Psychological Association
(800) 964-2000
www.helping.apa.org

National Center for Post Traumatic Stress Disorder
(802) 296-5132
www.ncptsd.org

National Alliance for the Mentally Ill
2107 Wilson Blvd., Ste. 300
Arlington, VA 22201
(800) 950-6264
www.nami.org

National Depressive and Manic-Depressive Association
730 N. Franklin St., Ste. 501
Chicago, IL 60610
(800) 826-3632
www.ndmda.org

National Institute of Mental Health
6001 Executive Blvd.
Room 81884, MSC 9663
Bethesda, MD 20892
(301) 443-4513
www.nimh.nih.gov

SEX ISSUES

Rape, Abuse and Incest
National Network
(800) 656-4673
www.rainn.org

National Council on Sexual Addiction and Compulsivity
P.O. Box 725544
Atlanta, GA 31139
(770) 541-9912
www.ncsac.org

SMOKING

Nicotine Anonymous World Services
419 Main St., PMB #370
Huntington Beach, CA 92648
(415) 750-0328
www.nicotine-anonymous.org

STRESS ISSUES

The Biofeedback & Psychophysiology Clinic
The Menninger Clinic
P.O. Box 829
Topeka, KS 66601-0829
(800) 351-9058
www.menninger.edu

New York Open Center
83 Spring St.
New York, NY 10012
(212) 219-2527
www.opencenter.org

The Stress Reduction Clinic Center for Mindfulness
University of Massachusetts
Medical Center
55 Lake Ave., North
Worcester, MA 01655
(508) 856-2656

TEEN

Al-Anon/Alateen
1600 Corporate Landing Parkway
Virginia Beach, VA 23454-5617
(888) 425-2666
www.al-anon.alateen.org

Planned Parenthood
810 Seventh Ave.
New York, NY 10019
(800) 230-PLAN
www.plannedparenthood.org

Hotlines for Teenagers
Girls and Boys Town National Hotline
(800) 448-3000

ChildHelp National Child Abuse Hotline
(800) 422-4453

Just for Kids Hotline
(888) 594-KIDS

National Child Abuse Hotline
(800) 792-5200

National Runaway Hotline
(800) 621-4000

National Youth Crisis Hotline
(800)-HIT-HOME

Suicide Prevention Hotline
(800) 827-7571

A Call For Authors

Most people have a story that needs to be shared. Could you be one of the contributing authors to be featured in an upcoming compilation book? As a result of becoming a Published Author, some of the Visionary Insight Press contributors are now writing and speaking around the world.

Visionary Insight Press is leading the industry in compilation book publishing and represent some of today's most inspirational teachers, healers and spiritual leaders.

Their commitment is to assist this planet we call "home" to be a place of kindness, peace and love. One of the ways they fulfill this promise is by assisting others with the sharing of their inspiring stories and words of wisdom.

They look forward to hearing from you.

Please visit

www.visionaryinsightpress.com